SPECTACULAR GOLF

AN EXCLUSIVE COLLECTION OF GREAT GOLF HOLES IN COLORADO

Foreword by Jack Nicklaus

Published by

PANACHE

PANACHE PARTNERS, LLC

13747 Montfort Drive, Suite 100
Dallas, Texas 75240
972.661.9884
Fax 972.661.2743
www.panache.com

Publishers: Brian G. Carabet and John A. Shand
Regional Publishers: Tom and Elizabeth Fischer
Contributing Editor: Michael Rabun
Designer: Mary Elizabeth Acree

Printed in Malaysia
Distributed by Independent Publishers Group
800.888.4741

PUBLISHER'S DATA

Spectacular Golf of Colorado
Library of Congress Control Number: 2006939717
ISBN 13: 978-1-933415-38-3
ISBN 10: 1-933415-38-X

First Printing 2007
10 9 8 7 6 5 4 3 2 1

Previous Page: The Bridges Golf & Country Club
See page 143 Photograph by Dick Durrance II

This Page: Lakota Canyon Ranch Golf Club
See page 181 Photograph by Dick Durrance II

INTRODUCTION

Inclement weather was obviously afoot on that early afternoon many years ago when our small collection of golfing enthusiasts stepped to the first tee at The Broadmoor.

The clouds were thick, there was a faint aroma of moisture in the air and those of us not familiar with the local meteorology were quickly becoming apprehensive.

No one, after all, enjoys having to abandon a long-planned day on the golf course—especially when that course is as resplendent as the jewel we were on the verge of challenging.

Fortunately, however, our host was well versed on the subject of Mother Nature and the way she works along the tumbling slopes that lead up to the nearby peaks.

"We might get a shower," he said. "But it won't last long."

There remained some hesitancy in our group.

"What about the fairways," someone said, expressing a clear tone of concern. "How long will it take them to get too wet to play?"

The gentleman who had invited us out for a day of recreation looked at the questioner as if he had just hurled the ultimate insult.

"Rain doesn't make these fairways wet," he said with mock disdain. "It just makes them greener."

Sure enough, before we could finish the first hole the light rain had come and gone. And, although it was difficult to say for sure, the assumption among us visitors was that the grass—an intense green to begin with—had taken on an ever-so-slightly darker hue than the one it had been displaying when the sun rose.

That, I have come to conclude over the decades, is the bottom line when it comes to playing golf in Colorado. It is all about visual intensity.

The colors are always so vivid. And not just the greens. There are rocks that, depending on the angle of the sun, can change from fiery red to deep maroon in short order. The wildflowers come in an assortment of shades, and all of them are brilliant.

Aspen in the autumn take on a color perhaps not found anywhere else. Out in the desert-like wilderness the earth tones abound in a variety that would tax an artist's palette.

And overseeing all of it are the mountains. If there is snow on them, it is a brilliant white. If not, we see the heavy gray normally associated with a battleship or sometimes the kind of deep blue that appears in an advancing thunderstorm.

Whatever the colors, they are singularly memorable, something you will be able to see for yourselves as you meander through the following pages.

Presented within this volume is Colorado golf at its flamboyant best. Dozens of courses will be seen in a variety of landscapes.

From these courses, in turn, are offered up what have been judged to be the most spectacular individual holes Colorado can offer.

In a pastime where differences of opinion are commonplace, it is assumed there might be those who would contend there have been flagrant omissions. But, as they say in this sport, "that's golf."

There can be no question, however, that remarkable scenes flourish within these covers—all the way from the lonely high plateaus down to the state's crowded hub of international commerce.

Everybody has a favorite, of course, and mine happens to be the closing hole at the Cherry Hills Country Club.

Golfers are not all that fond of mystery, and when one stands on Cherry Hills' 18th tee, there is no mystery at all. The task at hand is clearly spelled out, and it is also obvious that the task will not be your everyday assignment.

But there is more to it than that. History counts for a great deal in golf, and there is an awful lot of it associated with that particular hole.

Nevertheless, it must be admitted that while gathering data for this endeavor some challengers have taken their place on the personal list of favorites.

New courses have been developed during the opening years of the 21st century and more are appearing with each golfing season. There is staggering beauty to be found on these recent entries.

Invariably, though, the new Colorado courses share something with the ones that have been around for generations. Their colors are bright to the point of being luminous.

And even if the already bright green fairways do not actually deepen in color immediately after a rain, they should provide all those who take this golfing journey an abundance of very pleasurable viewing.

Michael Raburn

Editor

Castle Pines Golf Club 12th Hole

The Broadmoor 7th Hole, Mountain Course

FOREWORD

by Jack Nicklaus

I have always dealt my life's priorities in one simple hand: One, family; two, golf; three, business. Over the last couple of decades, numbers two and three have perhaps swapped places, but certainly for most of my life and career, I rarely shuffled the deck. There are special places that I have been with my family: memorable places I have golfed and spectacular places that I have worked that create a lasting memory for each of my life's priorities; but Colorado presents that rare opportunity to put everything into one frame.

I have always been an avid outdoorsman. I love to fish. I love to ski. I love to simply commune with nature. Colorado has for decades been among my favorite playgrounds. In fact, my family and I have always spent parts of our winters and even summers in Colorado, and to this day, we maintain a family getaway there.

If you had to trace my golf career back to one day that might be the genesis of all the wonderful things that have happened to me, you might rewind to 1959 and The Broadmoor in Colorado Springs. That is where, in the United States Amateur Championship, I defeated Charlie Coe—one of history's great amateur players and the defending champion—in a finals' match that was not decided until the last putt on the 36th and final hole. That victory at age 19 was my first national championship and served as a springboard to a career in which I have been very blessed.

I returned to Colorado the next year to taste championship golf on its highest level, when I was paired with Ben Hogan for the final 36 holes of the U.S. Open, which was played at Cherry Hills Country Club in Denver. I finished second, two shots back of my future rival and long-time friend Arnold Palmer, but to be just 20 and able to walk the fairways with one of golf's true legends taught me lessons that I was able to carry into the rest of my career. Ironically, if you fast-forward 33 years, I was able to return to Cherry Hills as a senior and win my second and final U.S. Senior Open Championship to provide a fitting bookend to my special connection to golf throughout the state of Colorado.

Just as the Champions Tour has given many professional golfers a second chance, golf course design has given me a second life. And few states represent my passion for the art of course design better than Colorado. By the end of 2006, my firm, Nicklaus Design, had been involved in a dozen courses open throughout the state—10 with which I have personally been involved. Each one has been a unique and special experience, because few settings and canvases are as spectacular as those you find in Colorado.

Whether it is the trees, streams, foliage or the rugged terrain of the mountains, nature always seems to determine what type of course I create. I have always kidded that Mother Nature is my co-designer, but in Colorado, she takes the lead. Anyone who has the opportunity to play in the state, whether they do so on a regular basis or as an occasional visitor, is fortunate in that they have a wide variety of wonderful golf courses from which to choose.

Golf is, at its foundation, the perfect opportunity for man to meet nature. As a player steps to the first tee and gazes out over a magnificent landscape that might feature a forest of pines, a fast-moving river or a snowcapped mountain peak (or perhaps all of that and more), the experience immediately becomes that much more pleasurable. This has always been the backdrop Colorado brings to the golf experience, whether that is in competition, as part of work or with your family by your side. Or in my case, all three.

Good golfing,

Photograph courtesy of Jack Nicklaus Foundation

COLORADO GOLF MAP

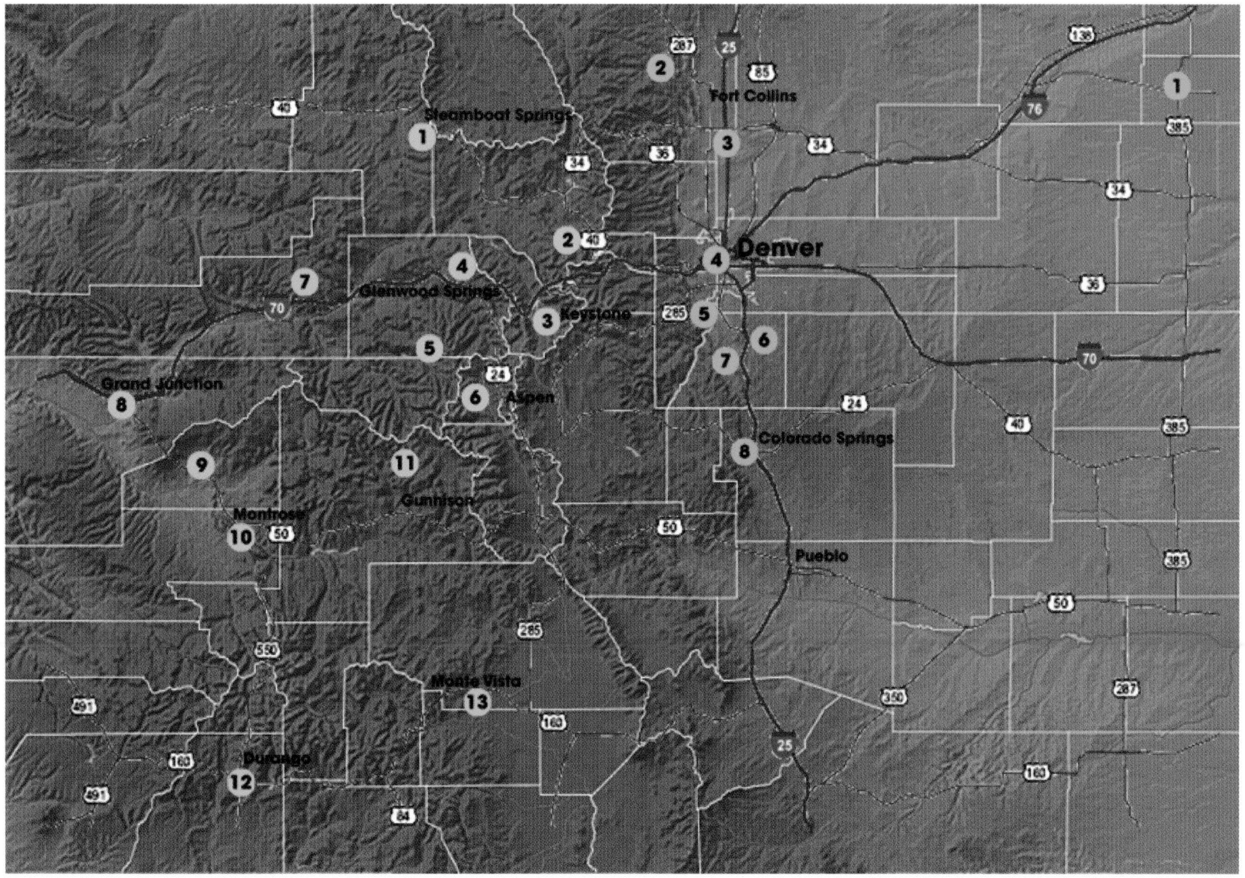

Denver Metro/Front Range

TABLE OF CONTENTS

Mountains

CHAPTER ONE

The Broadmoor 4th Hole, East Course

DENVER METRO/FRONT RANGE

Country Club at Castle Pines 18th Hole

Ballyneal 8th Hole

GOLF CLUB AT BEAR DANCE

2ND HOLE

218 yards • par 3

Larkspur, Colorado 303•681•4653 www.beardancegolf.com

Photographs by Julie Gibson

No sport pays homage to its history more than golf does and one is reminded of that fact every time a number is recorded on a scorecard at the Golf Club at Bear Dance.

The course is found just a few minutes off the busy interstate that links Colorado Springs and Denver and it creates an instant oasis from the hectic pace of life that the roadway symbolizes.

Each hole at Bear Dance is named for someone synonymous with golf and those names are listed on the scorecard. The second hole bears the name of the sport's first truly famous figure–Old Tom Morris.

Not only did he win four of the first eight British Opens, Old Tom did quite a bit of course designing. But he never had a piece of property to build a course on like the one that houses Bear Dance.

The test that carries his name is a magnificent short hole, although at 218 yards from the Pro Tee it can hardly be called short. In fact, the course as a whole measures a robust 7,726 yards. Fortunately, each hole has five sets of tees from which to choose.

At the second, however, any of the tees will present a challenge with a shot between the Ponderosa pines, over a waste area and past a cavernous bunker at the right, front corner of the green.

The left side of the green should be favored, not only to avoid the big bunker, but also to stay out of a deep swale that eats into the right portion of the putting surface.

The green slopes hard from left to right and a pot bunker can be found just beyond and to the left.

It makes for an all-encompassing examination with the sobering fact being that it is listed as the second-easiest hole on the course.

That would give any golfer, Old Tom Morris included, reason to contemplate what lies ahead.

THE BROADMOOR

4TH HOLE
East Course

166 yards • par 3

Colorado Springs, Colorado 719•577•5887 www.broadmoor.com

Photograph by Dick Durrance II

There is and always has been a special feel about the internationally famous grounds of The Broadmoor.

Those who see to the care and feeding of the property are able to create a quality of understated elegance around the place—especially on the golf course.

The grass seems to have a slightly thicker texture than one would expect. The evergreens look to be fuller than those found elsewhere. In a word, the whole scene looks "lush."

Broadmoor's East Course is known in the history of golf as the spot where both Jack Nicklaus and Annika Sorenstam won the first major titles of their careers—Nicklaus the 1959 U.S. Amateur and Sorenstam the 1995 U.S. Women's Open.

And over the years the course has become known for exquisite service and genteel surroundings.

Perhaps not enough attention, however, has been given to specific scenes that are found around this gem—one that was originally put together by architectural superstar Donald Ross.

The par-3 fourth hole is just such a scene, one that depicts what the course is all about.

It is not a particularly daunting hole, but it sits perfectly on the landscape in such a refined manner that it would not be out of place to see a sumptuous meal being served on the green.

But the hole does not allow for a so-so shot. A pond must be carried and the water is bordered by a rock face that adds a classy look to the picture.

Players travel across the water on another attractive feature that comes in the form of a stone bridge with black iron railings. The green itself falls away on all sides, which was Ross' best-known design feature, and a stand of trees directly behind the hole frames the view.

It may not do so immediately, but repeated playing of The Broadmoor will eventually force the thought to sink in. The charm and sophistication that is so prevalent within the walls of the hotel itself has, by design, spread out onto the golf course. And it is evident in every direction one cares to look.

CASTLE PINES

Golf Club

11TH HOLE

197 yards • par 3

Castle Rock, Colorado 303•688•6000 www.golfintl.com

Photograph by Dick Durrance II

Winding its way through rolling hillsides 25 miles south of Denver with grand views of the valley below and the Colorado Rockies beyond, Castle Pines Golf Club gives golfers the opportunity to enjoy the Mile High City's rarified air.

Prominent among the myriad of Castle Pines delights is this picture-perfect little gem, breathtaking in every sense, not the least of which is the meandering uphill hike from the 10th green through the pines and to the 11th's elevated tee.

It's not simply the 6,000-foot altitude–a Castle Pines hallmark–that makes the golfer breathless, but also the beauty of this marvelous little challenge.

The very deep, bi-level green nestles 75 feet below a quartet of tee areas, stretching 195 yards from the championship markers to the pin on the back shelf.

At first blush, it appears to be an invitation to make the birdies sing–particularly if you become distracted by the awesome floral display on the left bank leading to the Promised Land.

Poor planning would delude you into thinking this is where you get back at the course.

Gorgeous, towering pines frame the green, left, back and right, those on the right seemingly sitting smack dab in the center of the huge bunker that threatens to swallow a slightly tipsy or wind-caught shot.

If the trees are not barrier enough, a babbling brook tantalizingly meanders across the entire front of the green to claim the timid stroke.

It's a shot you can't take a pass on, but certainly a temptress of a par 3 you'd love to take a shot at with anything from a 5-iron to a wedge to a camera, all winds being equal–which they aren't.

You'll play a passel of par 3s before you'll find one more inviting than this one.

CHERRY HILLS

Country Club

12TH HOLE

207 yards • par 3

Englewood, Colorado 303•350•5200 www.chcc.com

Photograph by Jim Chiaffredo, Vincent Publishing, LLC

Cherry Hills Country Club is considered a test worthy of a major championship because when a title is on the line, shots of the highest quality are demanded down the stretch.

And although the focus invariably centers around the closing hole, there is a challenge early on the back nine that has always grabbed the attention of those doing the playing.

The par-3 12th has within its power the ability to make or break a championship run.

A long iron over water is not a pleasant prospect, especially when one considers that a shot hit with something less than perfection can lead to an instant double bogey and a likely relegation in the history book.

Under routine circumstances, it is a perfectly lovely hole. The tee-to-green pond sits there in all its tranquil beauty and the trees around the back of the green make for pleasant viewing while posing no threat.

But there is no way to escape the fact that the ball must leap off the clubface in order to achieve the desired result, which is a shot with loft and with spin that not only clears the water but also clears the slope between the water and the green.

Anything landing on the slope has a very good chance of bouncing back into the pond.

The prudent play is to take enough club to put the ball at least in the middle of the green and perhaps all the way to the back third.

When a championship is at stake, however, the pin will likely be placed near the front of the green, so if a birdie is needed the tee shot becomes that much more frightening.

Arnold Palmer, having fought his way into contention during the final round of the 1960 U.S. Open, made a safe par on the 12th as he began his march to an eventual championship.

Phil Mickelson had some breathing room when he came to the 12th hole during the title match of the 1990 U.S. Amateur, having taken a 3-up lead over Manny Zerman en route to a 5-and-4 victory.

But whether it is a friendly game with pals or the gut-wrenching closing stretch of a major championship with television cameras beaming images around the globe, the realization hits home at the 12th that the game of golf is about to serve up a classic challenge.

THE COUNTRY CLUB OF COLORADO

17TH HOLE

Photographs by Bob Smalley

187 yards • par 3

Colorado Springs, Colorado 719•538•4080 www.ccofcolorado.com

Water always seems to play a key role in the designs of Pete Dye.

The course for which he is best known—on which The Players Championship is contested each year—has water almost constantly in play. And the 17th hole on that course, with its island green, is now one of the most famous golfing spots in the world.

At The Country Club of Colorado's 17th hole, Dye has not recreated the island green. But water is certainly there and it is available in large quantities.

The flight path from the back tee to the front of the green is 100 percent carry—159 yards of it to be exact—and the water keeps going along the right edge of the putting surface.

There is a long bunker placed just to the left of the lake midway from tee to green and it can be a factor for a poorly hit shot from one of the forward tees.

For the most part, however, it is all about the water and the green, which would be hard enough to hit even if the lake was not standing there as such a sizeable guardian.

The green is shaped like an hourglass and at its narrowest point is only 14 yards wide. But it is almost half a football field in depth.

So The Country Club of Colorado's 17th hole contains the triple crown of golf. It forces the player to pick the right club, hit it in the air and hit it very, very straight.

Bunkers pinch in on both sides of the green at the waist of the hourglass, adding another roadblock to the successful completion of a hole that—because of the substantial amount of water—is instantly recognizable as being typical of a Pete Dye par 3.

DENVER
Country Club
5TH HOLE

188 yards • par 3

Denver, Colorado 303•733•2444 www.denvercc.net

Photograph courtesy of Denver Country Club

A venerable golf course located in the midst of a dense urban area is one of the few places where it is possible to truly feel as if one has stepped back in time.

Time, after all, is a major part of golf. It is a special treat to be able to walk along fairways where someone wearing a tie once struck the ball with a hickory-shafted club. In such locations, the trees have been there for generations.

Some holes are laid out much as they have been for decades, while others may have been revised or redesigned at some point in time. In either case, each evokes a rich history.

Such is the case at the Denver Country Club, which was founded two years after the 19th century came to an end.

That puts this facility well into its second hundred years, and the charming landscape does, indeed, serve as an oasis in the midst of the modern-day rush.

Tranquility is particularly evident when stepping onto the tee of the par-3 fifth, a hole that is so captivating it tends to divert one's attention from the business at hand.

The dominant feature of the hole is a picturesque pond that stretches from the tee to within a few steps of the green.

Not original to the hole, the pond was added in 1964 when the Club commissioned J. Press Maxwell and Johnny Cochran to redesign the fifth hole and several others.

Along with a new green, the revised hole incorporated the five-million-gallon reservoir out of necessity—the Club needed it to maintain its water rights.

While at-heart functional, the pond adds both beauty and challenge. The trees that grow along the edge of the water reflect their images onto it, creating yet another distraction for those who enjoy idyllic scenery with their golf.

Fairway-length grass to the right of the pond serves as an area of safety all the way up to the right-front corner of the green, but to get to the middle of the putting surface one must carry the water.

Two bunkers have been tucked between the green and the water on the left, and another bunker comes very much into play on the right as a penalty for those too timid to confront the pond.

The green wraps around the water and the two bunkers on the left side so that a back-left pin placement is supremely formidable.

Despite its difficulty, the fifth delights—the placid water and copious greenery make for an enchanting hole.

THE EISENHOWER

Golf Club

17TH HOLE

Blue Course

216 yards • par 3

Colorado Springs, Colorado 719•333•2606 www.eisenhowergolfclub.com

Photographs by Barry Staver

There is perhaps a no more complete collection of athletic venues on earth than the one found at the United States Air Force Academy.

Whatever the sport, it can be contested in the shadow of the Front Range. There is, for instance, a basketball arena, a hockey rink and an indoor track all under the same roof. There are acres and acres of green fields on which athletes have plied their trade since the Academy opened.

And then there is the golf.

The Eisenhower Golf Club is touted to be the best Department of Defense golf facility in the country, a reputation enhanced by the fact that there are 36 holes to enjoy.

The Silver and Blue courses fit in perfectly with the orderliness one would expect at a military academy. There are a series of spotless views that fall in line with the sharp edges of a cadet's uniform or the sharply angled spires of the landmark campus chapel.

One of the particularly tidy scenes is found at the par-3 17th on the Blue Course, which is a little longer and a little more difficult than its counterpart.

Even though the hole has considerable length, the green is an inviting target. No forced carry is needed so the player has an opportunity to bounce the ball onto the green, as long as it can find its way between the bunkers that guard the front corners of the putting surface.

It is the green itself that presents much of the challenge on this hole. Its left side consists of a shallow bowl. The green rises to a ridge on the right side and falls away again, creating a very difficult pin placement behind the right-hand bunker.

The pines that are ever present on the course stand in an appropriate formation around the green and only add to the neatness of the scene.

In the midst of a very special piece of American property on which the world of athletics counts for a lot, it soon becomes apparent that golf has been given its due.

FOX ACRES

Country Club

18TH HOLE

214 yards • par 3

Red Feather Lakes, Colorado 970•881•2191 www.foxacres.com

Photograph by Dick Durrance II

What began as a family getaway has, over the course of almost a half century, become a unique retreat where the woes of the outside world can be replaced by a multitude of entertaining outdoor activities, especially golf.

It is the Fox Acres Country Club, which began life as 38 pine-laden acres and a log cabin. The acreage has grown more than tenfold and the club now includes 15 lakes, trails for skiing and a fitness course on which exercise stations and equipment stand ready to help tone bodies and reduce waist sizes.

In short, Fox Acres is a refuge in which the splendors of nature can be absorbed in all the ways that can bring a family together–whether it be a day spent fishing, an early morning hike through a flowering meadow or the mere silent contemplation of the overwhelming serenity.

And for those who are addicted to the sport, there are also 18 holes that meander through the thick stands of pines to provide one of the most acclaimed golfing getaways in the state.

In addition to having a special allure, what with the ponds, the rock outcroppings and the trees that close in to form a barrier against the outside world, Fox Acres has the unusual feature of ending with a par 3.

Any architect that closes a course with a par 3 had best make that hole something to remember, and John Cochran, who spent 20 years developing the layout, did just that. The 18th, indeed, delivers a grand climax to the course.

No matter which of the five tees is used, a lake must be carried and even though there is a thin strip of grass between the water and the green, the ground slopes back down to the hazard.

So it is an all-carry shot to get to the putting surface, which is shaped roughly like a triangle and has three distinct levels. There are also four bunkers, all of which can come into play. Three of the traps are built into a slope behind the green and a shot from any of them could easily scurry back into the water.

The final problem is that the rustic, two-story clubhouse is located just behind the green, meaning any number of people might be watching as a struggling player attempts to complete play.

This hole would be well remembered no matter where it appeared in the round, but because it is the final hole it is especially hard to forget–just as is the case with the entire property.

HARMONY CLUB

12TH HOLE

160 yards • par 3

Timnath, Colorado 970•224•4622 www.harmonyclub.info

Photograph by Dick Durrance II

Those who are serious about golf believe the sport mirrors life, so it stands to reason that those who enjoy variety in their lives will find Harmony Club very much to their liking.

The brand-spanking-new course, designed by prolific architect Jim Engh, provides exceptional variety as part of a 640-acre development which, until recently, was the site of a nationally-recognized sheep ranch.

The course starts out in links style, then begins to weave through topographical changes and eventually provides visual drama of the first order. All the while there are the spectacular bunkers and mounding which are traits of an Engh layout.

There is another aspect of this course, however, that instantly comes to the attention of golfers who play all around Colorado.

It is commonplace to find various types of pines on the state's courses. And if there are no pines there are probably aspen. They are all glorious, but there is also a sameness. In a particular grove of pines, no matter the species, one tree looks pretty much like the rest.

At Harmony, each and every historic cottonwood has its own personality. The trees are referred to as "historic," because they were on the property longer than the sheep were—for more than 100 years.

Some of the most handsome specimen of cottonwood surround the green at the par-3 12th. As the tee shot is contemplated, it is the trees that catch the eye. They are tall, gnarled and display individual characteristics.

The green is built into a gentle hillside that slopes up and up beyond the target. Prairie grasses stand between the tee and green and also grow to the right of the intended path.

The ground all around the green tumbles and rolls and a sizeable pot bunker protects the very front middle of the putting surface. Lots and lots of items on which to fix your gaze.

And then there are the cottonwoods—each growing at its own angle, each with branches going their own direction and each one looking as if it could tell its own fascinating tale. The largest of them are to the left and behind the green. They are not really in the way, but they bring a special personality to a course where variety is the byword.

LAKEWOOD

Country Club

11TH HOLE

155 yards • par 3

Lakewood, Colorado 303•233•4614 www.lakewoodcountryclub.net

Photograph by Premier Aerials Photography

Although there has been an explosion of golf course construction in Colorado that matches just about any other spot in the country, the state has its share of historical sites as well.

The Lakewood Country Club sits at the forefront in that category.

During the first decade of the 21st century, Lakewood will celebrate its 100th birthday, and knitted into its lore are some of golf's most distinguished names.

Its original designer was Tom Bendelow, whose work can be found at the famed Medinah Country Club in suburban Chicago. When the course was expanded from nine to 18 holes, none other than Donald Ross was consulted. Past membership rolls include the name of Olympic and golfing superstar Mildred "Babe" Zaharias.

A course that has aged gracefully will include holes that can best be described as elegant and the 11th at Lakewood is just such a hole.

It is a par 3 that is not overly taxing, but which includes the classic elements that give the player pause before the tee shot is struck.

Lakewood's 11th plays from an elevated tee that usually causes one less club to be used than is normal for the distance.

A water hazard about 30 yards in depth fronts the green and, while it will obviously gather up a mishit shot, it provides as much scenic pleasure as it does golfing fright. The banks of the hazard are lined with rocks and a recently constructed stone bridge takes the player across the water.

Full-bodied willows to the left of the hole, both short and beyond the hazard, add to the view.

Two small bunkers are squeezed between the water and the two-level green and an imposing bunker is found just beyond the target. The large trap needs to be avoided because a shot from there could sail all the way over the green and back into the water.

In a sport where tradition plays such a large role, having a lineage that can be traced back a full century is a plus.

Lakewood has just such a lineage and, as the 11th hole demonstrates, it has the looks of a course that has properly ripened with age.

OMNI INTERLOCKEN

Resort Golf Club

2 ND HOLE

Eldorado Nine

142 yards • par 3

Broomfield, Colorado 303•438•6600 www.omnihotels.com

Photograph by Ken May, Rolling Greens Photography

After a pressurized business meeting in which various weighty decisions have been made, it is always nice to be able to step to the first tee and take part in 18 holes of unwinding.

There is a growing list of places that cater to both of those enterprises, and one is to be found on the way from Denver to Boulder.

The Omni Interlocken Resort provides all the desired amenities, whether the occasion is business or pleasure. Chief among those amenities, for those who are easily tempted by such a thing, are 27 holes of golf.

The three nine-hole courses—Eldorado, Vista and Sunshine—were designed by David Graham, who in 1981 hit every green in the final round at the revered Merion Golf Club and won the U.S. Open by three shots.

If the Eldorado Nine is part of the day's play, there will be an early encounter with a green that is difficult to hit even by Graham's standards.

Those familiar with this facility believe that the hardest club selection to make on any of the 27 holes comes at the Eldorado Nine's par-3 second.

Length is certainly not a problem. This is a short hole—even from the back tee.

Accuracy is the key since a pond laps up to the front-edge of the triangle-shaped green and continues along the entire right side.

There is a refuge of short grass to the left of the water and to the left of the green: Those with a good short game will have a reasonable chance to save par from that location.

The only bunker on the hole is to the back right of the green and is not all that much of a factor.

It all comes down to how bold a player wants to be in a bid for birdie, which on a hole this short is within the realm of possibility even for those with marginal skills. But those who do choose the bold route had best select the proper club.

THE CLUB AT PRADERA

15TH HOLE

189 yards • par 3

Parker, Colorado 303•607•5700 www.theclubatpradera.com

Photograph by Jim Engh

When surveying the upcoming shot, those who have become fairly adept at golf will first consider the following question:

"Where is the best place to miss it?"

The good golfers are always thinking ahead. On the assumption that this shot does not go in the hole, which is usually a good assumption, where is the most agreeable spot from which to hit the next one?

The trouble with a well-designed par 3 is that there is quite often nowhere good to miss it. If the tee shot is not a good one, there is plenty of trouble to pay.

That is the case with the fourth of the five par 3s at The Club at Pradera. It is also the shortest par 3 on the course and, it probably should go without saying, is pleasing to the eye.

The hole sits in an oversized dell with the tees placed on the side of a hill and with the ground rising up behind and to the right of the green.

Located down in the hollow is the green and languishing between the tee and the green, several feet below the level of the putting surface, are the blue waters of a placid pond.

It is, in other words, all carry—unless one takes advantage of a tiny bail-out area short and right of the green—from which a par becomes more of a wish than a likelihood.

In fact, a shot that comes to rest anywhere other than on the green presents problems.

A ridge with thick grass runs behind the green, serving as a backdrop to the entire scene. An oversized pot bunker takes up space between the water and the front of the green. Another bunker has been created beyond the green, built into one more slope that sweeps up above the short grass.

The extreme right side of the green falls away toward the bail-out area and needs to be avoided.

As it turns out, there are lots and lots of spots to be avoided when playing this hole, although there is no refuting that those spots are easy on the eye.

THE GOLF CLUB AT RAVENNA

9TH HOLE

230 yards • par 3

Denver, Colorado 720•956•1600 www.ravennagolf.com

Photograph by Ken May, Rolling Greens Photography

Those who watch a fair amount of golf on television will ultimately hear an announcer give the following critique of a player's swing:

"It is clear he wanted to take the right side out of play."

Whatever it is that a player does to take the right side out of play should be studied and committed to memory before taking on the par-3 ninth hole at Ravenna, the gorgeous course that has recently grown out of the stony ground southwest of Denver.

Ravenna's front nine ends with a one-shot hole that is typically striking but which is also long. Even the tees utilized by the average player force a shot that requires more length than is normally called for on a par 3.

In such cases, architects usually create a lot of room in front of the green so that the ball can run onto the short grass. And course designer Jay Morrish has done just that with this hole.

Additionally, there is quite a bit of open space to the left of the green as well. There is no water to the left and no enormous bunker. Even the slope of the land works to the golfer's advantage. The mounding to the left of the green can cause the ball to bounce back toward the putting surface and maybe even onto it.

The forgiving nature to be found short of and to the left of the green is a welcome sight for those who rarely are able to pull off a towering 200-yard shot that lands softly near the hole location.

There is, however, one clearly labeled "no go" area. It is very unwise to hit it right at Ravenna's ninth hole.

A series of bunkers take up space along the right side from short of the green to almost all the way to the back of it. They are there as a form of prevention—to catch a ball and keep it from bounding down a steep slope into an unfriendly area of tall grass and shrubs.

Morrish, one of the most accomplished designers in the business, always gives players a chance. On this hole, despite its length, he has built in plenty of room in which to maneuver the ball. None of that maneuvering room, however, is located to the right.

THE RIDGE

at Castle Pines North

17TH HOLE

175 yards • par 3

Castle Rock, Colorado 303•688•0100 www.theridgecpn.com

Photograph courtesy of Troon Golf

The eyes cannot stay focused on one thing for long at a course designed by Tom Weiskopf.

There is just too much to see. His works are often like a grand opera. All those spear carriers on the stage might be standing silent while the tenor is belting out a big number, but the audience certainly takes notice of them.

The Ridge at Castle Pines North, a Troon Golf-managed facility, indeed, provides a lot to see, including the ridge that separates the two nines and gives the course its name.

There is a particularly stunning distraction at the par-3 17th, a hole that has been chiseled out of rock outcroppings.

The five tees, which allow the hole to be played at distances ranging from 175 down to 86 yards, have been placed in a funnel of trees, rocks and underbrush that create a visual diversion all by themselves.

But the chief attraction is off in the distance—beyond and above the green.

It is a large chunk of stone that bears some resemblance to nearby Castle Rock, the huge crag that rises high above the land and can be seen for great distances.

This landscape feature at the 17th hole, however, is embedded in the earth and actually has the 18th tee built on top of it.

The 17th green rests directly below the rock, and those two elements are connected by a mound that is covered on its upper half by natural growth and on its lower half by carefully manicured grass.

It is a unique scene which can easily cause the concentration to stray. That would not be good because the tee shot to a slightly elevated green must clear three bunkers and come to rest on a shallow, wide target.

All manner of hard-to-negotiate putts might be encountered before escaping with a par, after which the eyes can roam around one more time to take in the many sights of another Weiskopf kaleidoscope.

SANCTUARY

10TH HOLE

206 yards • par 3

Sedalia, Colorado 303•224•2860 www.sanctuarygolfcourse.com

Photograph by Dick Durrance II

The character of a par 3, no matter where it is, always seems to be heightened when it is located in an amphitheater setting.

There cannot be too many amphitheater settings more imposing than the one that houses the 10th at Sanctuary—the unique course devoted to the preservation of wildlife and the work of charitable causes.

Just by itself, the hole is a wonderful example of golf architecture. The green presents a sizeable target, but when it is missed, the surrounding perils can quickly inflate the stroke total.

What sets this hole apart, however, is what lies beyond the reach of even the longest of tee shots.

Over there—about 30 miles away—and very much within eyesight is the Front Range. Pikes Peak rises up beyond that, easily visible on a clear day despite the fact it would take about 500 perfectly struck 2-irons to reach its base.

The 10th green at Sanctuary contains 7,840 square feet of putting surface, making it the largest on the course. The right-hand third of the green falls off into a lower level and is separated by a ridge that runs from front to back.

Just getting on the green, therefore, by no means guarantees a par. But getting on the green is certainly more preferable than not getting on it.

To the left of the green is an impressive mound about 10 feet high with a solitary pine sticking out of it. A multi-fingered bunker sits below the right-front corner of the green with the putting surface wrapping around it.

If a ball comes to rest on the very front of the green and the hole is cut in the back-right portion, it becomes impossible to putt directly at the hole.

Such are the complexities that exist at Sanctuary's 10th, although the view from the tee tends to make what happens during the playing of the hole pretty much irrelevant.

VALLEY

Country Club

4TH HOLE

179 yards • par 3

Aurora, Colorado 303•690•6373 www.valleycountryclub.org

Photographs by Premier Aerials, LLC

The vast majority of golfing hazards, whether they involve sand, water, plant life or the subtleties in the way the land moves, are found along the ground.

On occasion, however, golfers run into an obstacle that takes up air space.

There is just such a hindrance at the Valley Country Club, located adjacent to the southern edge of the Cherry Creek State Recreation Area.

Cherry Creek itself, a major player in Denver's heritage, runs through the course. And there is water in play at the par-3 fourth hole, although it is not part of Cherry Creek.

Instead, it comes in the form of a pond, but it is not always the most troublesome peril on the hole.

Ten yards short of the green and just left of the direct route to the middle of the putting surface is a large cottonwood. If the flagstick is located on the left half of the green, therefore, it is blocked out by the tree.

That, in turn, means the tee ball must be lofted over the tree or brought around it by means of a right-to-left shot.

If there is a collision between the ball and the cottonwood, the best that can happen is that the ball will drop straight down and the player will have a clear swing for a pitch to the green.

The worst that can happen is that the ball will ricochet into the water and the whole process will have to start over again.

There are also three bunkers, two fairly deep ones in front and a shallow one that has been placed into a slope behind the green. And the green also tilts a little from back to front, enough so that a putt from beyond the pin cannot be struck all that aggressively.

The Valley Country Club has been in business for more than a half century, and during that time the cottonwood at the fourth hole has batted down many a shot.

That means it has caused much consternation in its day. And there is no doubt much more of it is to come.

BALLYNEAL

14TH HOLE

362 yards • par 4

Holyoke, Colorado 970•854•5900 www.ballyneal.com

Photograph by Dick Durrance II

Ballyneal, the stunning new course created among the dunes in the northeastern corner of Colorado, is built on ground relatively devoid of landmarks.

From start to finish, Ballyneal provides a dazzling reminder of golf as it was played in its earliest days. Humps and hollows litter the fairways, the sand hills are always lurking to absorb mis-directed shots and the wind that never seems to blow in the same direction for two consecutive days helps create a different experience each time out.

The 14th hole demonstrates all that while also showing us how a stark landscape can be synonymous with beauty.

It is a short par 4 that, thanks to the design work of Tom Doak, has an intimidating look while obscuring the safest route to the green.

From the tee, the chief hazards are clearly visible. There is a complex of bunkers at the corner of the dogleg as the hole makes a slight turn to the left. There is also a bunker in the middle of the tumbling fairway and it can be reached from the back tee with a shot of about 250 yards.

The prudent play would be to stay short of that bunker. The bold play would be to flirt with the corner of the dogleg in an attempt to drive past all the trouble.

But there is another route, which when the hole is being played for the first time is not clearly evident. The right side of the fairway, hidden by one of the course's countless dunes, contains an ample landing area. A tee shot to the right leaves a longer second, but on a hole that is not all that long to begin with, safety is a very viable option.

The green is protected on the left by a dune and a shot that comes up even the slightest bit short will tumble back into one of the two hollows just in front of the putting surface.

At first glance, it would appear best to err on the side of long with the approach. But the back of the green slopes away and a ball that sails past the middle portion tends to bounce back into another swale.

There is not a bunker to be found around this green. Instead, its defense is the land itself, thus creating a challenge that is full of the subtleties that hark back to the game's origins.

It is a lofty legacy to aim for, but it is one that Ballyneal has achieved.

THE GOLF CLUB AT BEAR DANCE

Photographs by Julie Gibson

6TH HOLE

353 yards • par 4

Larkspur, Colorado 303•681•4653 www.beardancegolf.com

It is customary to find a golf course's logo displayed at the establishment's front entrance, on the stationery and on the napkins in the grill.

The Golf Club at Bear Dance, however, manages to do something a lot more imaginative than that.

Its logo is the imprint of a bear paw and on the line directly between the tee and the green at the sixth hole is a replica of the logo—created as a real life hazard in the form of 11 bunkers.

From ground level, the traps appear to be nothing more than an inconvenient grouping of sand-filled holes conjured up by an architect who wanted to spice up a short par 4.

From above, however, an obvious pattern emerges. The collection of traps perfectly depicts the logo. A wide bunker simulates the pad of the bear's paw and the 10 smaller traps, in two rows, are emblematic of the claws.

The traps can take their place among the most unique hazards in the country, joining such notables as the Churchpew Bunkers at Oakmont in Pennsylvania and the Mickey Mouse Bunker at Walt Disney World's Magnolia Course in Florida.

The whole Bear's Paw complex is easily visible from the elevated tee and because the sixth hole is short on length (only 315 yards from the middle of the five tees), the sand is reachable with a big drive.

There is a lot of fairway out to the left, however, and a sensible shot directed away from the Bear's Paw will leave a mere pitch uphill to the shallow green. Even so, the approach will likely have to carry a portion of the sand, which in addition to being a symbol for the course seems to act as a magnet for golf balls.

Each of the holes on the course is named for a famous golfing figure and the sixth, naturally, is called, "The Bear," in honor of Jack Nicklaus.

The ingenious design work and the tribute to the game's history could make for pleasant conversation topics as players prepare to play the sixth. A visit to the Bear's Paw, however, could easily turn the conversation into something other than congenial.

THE BROADMOOR

18TH HOLE
East Course

415 yards • par 4

Colorado Springs, Colorado 719•577•5887 www.broadmoor.com

Photograph by Dick Durrance II

For a closing hole to be truly memorable, it needs to provide a memorable view.

And the scene that is there for the viewing from the middle of the 18th fairway of The Broadmoor's East Course is one that will easily stick in the brain cells.

The course provides a challenging conclusion that has tested superbly skilled players down through the years. The 16th is a solid par 3 and the 17th is a long par 5 that requires the straightest shots a player can muster.

And then comes a conclusion that is fitting for a golf course on which shot values and scenic values go hand in hand.

The tee shot must carry out to the spot where the fairway makes a right-hand turn so that there is a clear look available for the approach.

And what a look it is.

First there is the water that must be carried with the second shot. If the tee shot has reached the proper point, carrying the water is not all that formidable a task. But it is a task, nevertheless.

Then there is the green beyond, rolling up and over a ridge so as to provide putting challenges of the first order. A bunker eats into the right side of the green and all around is the perfectly manicured grass befitting the stylish image that is synonymous with The Broadmoor.

And then there is the structure that dominates the landscape—a multi-story, multi-purposed, sprawling building that looks to have been recently lifted from somewhere along the Mediterranean coast.

It is certainly imposing, but it needs to be looked at in sections for a full architectural appreciation—from the orange roofing tiles to the adobe façade to the tall watchtower and its ornate clock.

There is all that white trim around the floor-to-ceiling windows. And the expansive green and white awning tends to become a center of attention.

The scene visible from the 18th fairway absolutely reeks of memorable character which, when mixed with golf, turns out to be what The Broadmoor is all about.

CASTLE PINES

Golf Club

10TH HOLE

485 yards • par 4

Castle Rock, Colorado 303•688•6000 www.golfintl.com

Photograph by Dick Durrance II

Arguably the most beautiful, inarguably the most difficult hole at the Jack Nicklaus-designed Castle Pines Golf Club is the 10th.

Breathtaking in every way, the hole starts at an elevated tee box, sweeps downhill through the pines and over the lake and culminates with a huge green of fiendish delights and disappointments.

One of the most cussed and discussed holes on the PGA Tour, it has proved to be the most difficult in 18 of the first 21 International Tournaments, ranging from an average of 4.27 in 1991 to 4.52 strokes in 1995.

The generous fairway is framed by giant pines on a hillside to its left and a shelf that drops into gnarly rough to the right.

Cradled in another hillside and deceptively sloping from back to front, the green is hugged from the left corner to the back right by a frontal lake.

The hole's only two bunkers swallow overly aggressive shots and afford scary, ski-jump looks toward the water on the escape route.

The ideal fairway landing area affords a spectacular view of the majestic Pikes Peak behind the green, though 45 miles distant, and while it's 450 yards away, Tour gargantuan Hank Kuehne once found the lake with his 3-wood tee shot.

Colorado's rarified air, the downhill slope and Kuehne's brute force formed a formidable troika—but 450 yards!

The 10th has been cussed and discussed enough that many Tour players would have preferred to take a fifth.

Punctuating just how both delightful and confounding it can be are experiences by South African stylist Ernie Els. The Big Easy's only International win came in 2000 on the strength of an eagle two—worth five points—on the 10th, one of only three in history there; but he also lost it by two points twice when he double-bogied it—minus three points.

CASTLE PINES

Golf Club

18TH HOLE

480 yards • par 4

Castle Rock, Colorado 303•688•6000 www.golfintl.com

Photograph by Dick Durrance II

When Castle Pines Golf Club founder Jack Vickers launched The International Tournament in 1986, he unveiled two eye-popping innovations—the most unique scoring format in the PGA Tour's storied history as well as the first announced million-dollar purse.

The game's premier players have experienced an altogether fascinating sudoku-like scoring format modified from the United Kingdom's Stableford system, accumulating points instead of calculating their scores in relation to old man par.

The premium is placed on a sub-par score each hole, which encourages risk-taking but with definite risk-reward consequences.

A birdie is worth two points, an eagle is worth five and the rare double eagle, or albatross, is worth eight. But a bogey causes a point to be taken away and a double bogey or worse results in a deduction of three points.

So if a player comes to the 18th hole on the final round with a four-point advantage over the nearest competitor already finished, he's home free because the most he can lose is three points.

Year in and year out, the 18th has proved a stern final-day test that can fray nerves if a par is needed to win.

Punctuating the excitement of the tournament's format is this little mind-boggler: The International is the only event in golf in which a player could come to the 72nd hole and win with a birdie and lose with a par—go figure.

The landing area on 18 cannot be seen from the tee, but there is a flagpole on the right hillside that serves as a guide.

From the plateau fairway, the second shot is downhill to a large, multi-level green strategically protected by bunkers in front, to the right and behind.

The imposing clubhouse and its distinctive clock tower awaits beyond the 18th green, holding a locker room consistently voted by the players as the best on the PGA Tour.

The 18th has been the site of past International champions such as Vijay Singh, Ernie Els, Greg Norman and two-time winners Phil Mickelson and Davis Love III, demonstrating that the best players in the game enjoy the change of pace as well as Castle Pines' remarkable ambience.

COUNTRY CLUB AT CASTLE PINES

4TH HOLE

458 yards • par 4

Castle Rock, Colorado 303•688•7400 www.ccatcastlepines.com

Photograph by Bevan & Jane Hardy, Shotmakers Photography

The Castle Pines Golf Club, host of a PGA Tour event each year, sits partway up a miniature mountain and has typically breathtaking views of the earth below.

Amazingly enough, there are 18 more holes even higher on the same slope. They make up the Country Club at Castle Pines, a course that can rival just about any other in the matter of elevation changes.

The second shot at the par-4 ninth, for instance, goes straight up. The tee shot at the par-4 10th goes straight down. And throughout the course there are shots required which bear the unmistakable stamp of designer Jack Nicklaus.

After beginning at the tip top of the property on the opening tee, the golfer travels a generally downhill path through the first three holes and the thought would then be that surely there have to be some uphill shots coming up pretty soon.

Not yet.

The tee at the par-4 fourth sits far above the fairway, offering a lovely view of the green target below.

But there is a twist to this hole. Located in the middle of all that green is a splash of white in the form of a bunker. It sits right in the middle of the fairway, and for most players it is unreachable.

The trap serves as an aiming point and it is a unique golfing thrill to hit an excellent shot off the tee and watch the ball as it hangs in the air for a very long time before plopping down comfortably short of the hazard.

For those long enough to reach the bunker, there is a choice of either hitting it to the left of the sand (where there is a little more room than to the right) or taking a lesser club than driver.

A solid shot will leave a short iron to a green that is protected in the left-front by a bunker and on the right by a tightly mown chipping area. Mounds of grass surround the green complex and giant trees encompass the hole from tee to green.

On a course filled with ups and downs, some of them quite dramatic, the fourth provides an excellent example of the latter.

COUNTRY CLUB AT CASTLE PINES

18TH HOLE

386 yards • par 4

Castle Rock, Colorado 303•688•7400 www.ccatcastlepines.com

Photograph by Dick Durrance II

The final hole at the Country Club at Castle Pines goes uphill. Considering the surrounding countryside, there wasn't anywhere else for it to go.

A round at this Jack Nicklaus-designed course features elevation changes of the first order and the 18th is no exception. It provides a final compromise with the severe slopes onto which the course was placed.

There are two major features visible from the tee. One is a pond, which is not really in play but which adds to the beauty of the hole. The other is a wall of pine trees sitting on the slopes that tower above and beyond the fairway as it makes a turn to the left.

It is not unlike playing golf in a gorge, except this one contains neatly trimmed grass instead of boulders and rushing water.

Those who hit the ball a considerable distance can aim a little left off the tee and cut off some yardage for their second shot. But anything in the fairway should be considered worthwhile. From the back tee it takes a shot of about 240 yards to carry over rough and a grass bunker to reach the fairway.

It is a distinctly uphill haul from the tee out to the fairway. But the second shot is even more so, forcing an extra club or two to be taken into consideration.

There are no bunkers around the green, which sits in a slight bowl, has three levels and is one of the most difficult on the entire course. And because of the elevation change, the final full shot of the day is to a target that cannot be fully seen.

Once play has been completed, the severity of the slope becomes evident one more time.

Even though the 18th hole is dramatically uphill, it does not begin to bring the players back to the clubhouse. The drive (no one would want to walk it) from the 18th green up to the gorgeous club headquarters is substantial.

And from there awaits a view that makes the trip very well worth it.

THE COUNTRY CLUB OF COLORADO

14TH HOLE

386 yards • par 4

Colorado Springs, Colorado 719•538•4080 www.ccofcolorado.com

Photographs by Bob Smalley

Pete Dye is the unquestioned master at making a golf hole look harder than it really is, although there is the added fact that most of the holes he designs are pretty hard in the first place.

The Country Club of Colorado, found at the base of imposing Cheyenne Mountain, is a Dye product and it serves up the sort of challenges typically created by one of the best-known architects in the history of the game.

The course has become known for being immaculately manicured, and the greens have undulations to test the best of short games. Those greens are also kept at a professional pace.

There is usually ample room on the fairways, however, as long as the player does not try to overstep his or her personal skill level.

A perfect example is the par-4 14th, where it becomes crucial not to bite off more than one can chew.

The hole is not a long one, but it doglegs to the right, and a lake fills the entire inside corner of the dogleg and extends all the way behind and to the right side of the green.

So an obvious decision must be made as to how much of the water can be cleared with the tee shot. The farther right the ball travels, thus cutting down the distance for the second shot, the longer the ball must stay in the air to get over the lake.

Those who can carry it 300 yards, and there are actually some who can, might even have a go at the green in one massive blast.

But the sensible approach is to aim well left to reduce the impact created by the liquid hazard. Any decent shot that reaches the fairway will leave a less-than-brutal approach, so long as that approach does not drift to the right or too long and find the water.

The green has two levels and is protected both in the front and behind by bunkers. The biggest test of all, though, comes on the tee—where the player must have the mental strength to stay away from the heroic shot when a heroic shot is not needed.

It is the kind of test that comes early and often at courses designed by Pete Dye.

CHERRY CREEK

Country Club

5TH HOLE

432 yards • par 4

Denver, Colorado 303•597•0300 www.cherrycreekcountryclub.com

Photograph by Premier Aerials Photography

There has been so much golf course construction around the outskirts of Denver during the last generation that at times the area seems to be one giant par 5.

In the early years of the 21st century, however, a course and surrounding home sites were developed right in the midst of the city. And none less than Jack Nicklaus did the design work.

It is the Cherry Creek Country Club and it is surprising, indeed, to find such a newly-minted course in such an ultra-urban setting.

Among other things, Nicklaus was an extraordinary mid-iron player and his courses usually demand solid iron play. Such is the case at Cherry Creek's par-4 fifth, where an expanse of sand dominates the scene.

The tee shot is fairly straightforward, although a grove of tall trees on the left side reduces the sight line for the drive. It takes a poor shot to find the trees, which are found only a short distance in front of the tee, but they can serve as a distraction.

Beyond the trees and to the left of the fairway soon appears the sand, created as a waste area. It remains in play all the way to the green and along the left side of it as well.

Two islands of rough ground have been left within the sand, and those islands have pine trees growing out of them.

The sand is maintained much as the bunkers are, but as an officially designated waste area it is permissible to ground the club while trying to extricate a ball from it.

The green is deep, narrow and has two distinct levels, making it a difficult target to hit—especially with all that sand lurking there waiting for a shot that makes the slightest of turns to the left. A regulation bunker is also placed on the right-front corner of the green and another is found on the back right.

It all leads to the necessity for an outstanding iron shot, which should come as no surprise when the name Nicklaus is involved.

CHERRY HILLS

Country Club

1 ST HOLE

Photographs by Jim Chiaffredo, Vincent Publishing, LLC

404 yards • par 4

Englewood, Colorado 303•350•5200 www.chcc.com

Early on the afternoon of June 18, 1960, Arnold Palmer walked out of the Cherry Hills Country Club dining room in anger because a long-time newspaper friend had just sarcastically told him he was too far behind with one round to play to win the U.S. Open.

Palmer, having left half his lunch uneaten, hit a few practice balls, then stalked to the first tee and proceeded to hit one of the most famous shots in the history of golf.

It was the moment that put Cherry Hills on the sport's historical map.

The final round of the 1960 U.S. Open is usually summed up in just a few words. Palmer drove the green at the 346-yard, par-4 first hole, recorded four birdies in a row to start the round, shot a 65, made up a seven-shot deficit and won his first and only U.S. Open title by two shots over a chubby-cheeked, 20-year-old amateur named Jack Nicklaus.

There was so much more to it than that, of course. As many as a dozen people had a chance to win the tournament as the final round played out—including Ben Hogan, Julius Boros and third-round leader Mike Souchak.

But it was Palmer who prevailed, celebrating the sinking of his final putt by taking off his visor and throwing it as high as he could. That scene was captured on film and is often seen when golf's great achievements are remembered.

Only a few spectators, however, saw Palmer's first shot of the round. From an elevated tee, the ball was blasted between the rows of trees that create such a narrow driving area. It landed well short of the green but had so much velocity remaining that it burned along the fairway, hopped through the thick collar of grass in front of the green, and ran 20 feet past the hole.

From there, Palmer left his eagle attempt four feet short. But he holed the remaining putt, and four hours of golf history had begun.

The hole now plays almost 60 yards longer than it did then, and the tee has been moved back into a narrow chute. But with a bunker on the left side of the fairway and a stream on the right, it presents the same sort of challenge it did when Palmer made sure the first hole at Cherry Hills would always have its place in the annals of the sport.

CHERRY HILLS

Country Club

18TH HOLE

491 yards • par 4

Englewood, Colorado 303•350•5200 www.chcc.com

Photograph by Jim Chiaffredo, Vincent Publishing, LLC

The closing hole at the Cherry Hills Country Club is played by its members as a par 5. But because its distance allows it to be reached in two by players with professional skills, it is listed as a par 4 when major championships come to call.

And what a par 4 it is—one worthy of being the finishing hole for any major event ever played.

The view from the tee instantly lets us know what major championship pressure is all about. There is water not only directly in front of the tee but all up the left side of the fairway. And the undulating fairway slopes from right to left so dramatically that it almost looks like a dart board off in the distance.

So the questions abound on the tee. How much of the water can be carried with the drive? Should the tee ball be struck with a left-to-right action, which would be relatively safe but would be a shot that bores into the slope of the fairway and be robbed of distance? Or should it be right-to-left, a shot that, if overdone, could escape down the slope to an almost certain watery finish?

Ben Hogan hit his tee shot in the water on this hole during the final round of the 1960 U.S. Open, eliminating him from contention. There is a classic picture of Tommy Bolt in the act of heaving his driver toward the water during that same tournament after his tee ball took a dive.

And even after the perfect drive there is the uphill second to a green protected by huge bunkers at the front corners.

Four is a daunting score to have to make for a championship.

Arnold Palmer made a four on the 72nd hole in 1960 to post a two-shot victory. Andy North needed "only" a bogey at the closing hole in 1985 to win the U.S. Open, and he wound up making a nervous, sharply breaking four-foot putt to secure that bogey.

When the U.S. Women's Open was contested at Cherry Hills in 2005, Birdie Kim of South Korea came to the closing hole tied with 17-year-old amateur Morgan Pressel. Kim put her second shot into a bunker and then, with Pressel watching from the fairway, holed her third for, appropriately enough, a birdie.

Pressel eventually bogeyed the hole and finished two shots back.

Drama is what one wants at the conclusion of a big-time tournament and the 18th at Cherry Hills is the perfect hole to fulfill those expectations.

COLUMBINE

Country Club

5TH HOLE

343 yards • par 4

Columbine Valley, Colorado 303•794•6333 www.columbinecountryclub.org

Photograph by Premier Aerials Photography

When Don January was among the PGA Tour's more consistent performers, he always had the perfect disposition for golf.

"Just because you miss the green," he would say in his syrupy voice, "doesn't mean you can't make a par." And, having said that, he would amble off with just enough speed to outrace a snail.

January won one major title in his career, and it came in 1967 at the Columbine Country Club, where he birdied three of the last five holes to tie fellow-Texan Don Massengale and then defeated Massengale by two shots in an 18-hole playoff to capture the PGA Championship.

Columbine, one of the state's historic golfing treasures, has recently undergone a major overhaul, but the theme of the course is unchanged from the day January walked off the 18th green as a major champion.

It is a narrow layout that requires preciseness rather than brute strength. And nowhere does preciseness come in more handy than at the par-4 fifth.

Since the hole measures less than 350 yards and because a man-made pond surrounds the green, care has to be given to make sure the ball is not hit too far. Something less than a driver is ordinarily used from the tee and those capable of crushing it have even been known to have a go at the green with one heroic blow.

The normal play is to leave an approach shot in the 100-yard range, but in addition to delivering the proper distance off the tee, it is necessary to deliver the proper line as well. Although there are not a lot of trees on the hole, there are enough of them on both sides of the fairway so that they can get in the way of the second shot if the first one has strayed off line.

Having to merely chip the ball back in the fairway when the target is so near represents true aggravation.

Although the hole has an island green, it is a fairly big island. So if the approach misses the green by a few feet there is still a chance to stay out of the water. There is more dry land past the green than there is left, right or short.

So, just as January was always reminding us, missing the green at Columbine's fifth does not necessarily mean a par cannot be saved. As long as the ball stays out of the pond, that is.

OMNI INTERLOCKEN

Resort Golf Club

4TH HOLE

Sunshine Nine

337 yards • par 4

Broomfield, Colorado 303•438•6600 www.omnihotels.com

Photograph by Dan Brace

The whole purpose at a resort golf course is to provide those who play it a really, really good time.

Players of average skills do not want to have to face the kind of challenges they might find at the U.S. Open. They want a well-prepared course on which they can have at least a reasonable amount of success.

The Omni Interlocken's three nine-hole courses in suburban Denver are made to order for the resort player. In the language of the game, these courses give the player a chance.

The fourth hole on the Sunshine Nine is a case in point. It is a short par 4 that looks intimidating but can be conquered with shots that do not need to be Herculean.

From the tee the eyes are assaulted by long grass, a bunch of bunkers and a ravine that travels down the left side of the fairway and then makes a right turn in front of the green. It is altogether threatening in appearance.

Out there in the middle of all that is the landing area—not particularly large but not all that far away, either. The fairway angles in such a way that a series of three bunkers must be carried to reach the short grass. But the ball needs to stay short of three more bunkers on the far side of the fairway.

Even the mid-handicap player who is used to automatically pulling out a driver might have to rethink what club to use off this tee.

Once a precise shot is executed, the chore becomes to loft a short iron over the ravine onto a multi-tier green that does not have a single bunker protecting it. But if the green is missed, the ball can easily nestle down into longish grass, and from there the odds are against saving a par.

The grassy hillsides into which these courses are set surround the scene but do not come into play. Instead, they encase a series of holes that provide an opportunity for what all golfers hope to find—a little well-earned success.

THE GOLF CLUB AT RAVENNA

Photographs by Ken May, Rolling Greens Photography

7TH HOLE

341 yards • par 4

Denver, Colorado 720•956•1600 www.ravennagolf.com

Land that the pioneers might have considered to be unappealing and sinister is now usually looked upon as much-in-demand real estate and it is on just such a plot of ground that Ravenna has been created.

Famed golf course architect Jay Morrish chiseled 18 unforgettable holes out of the rock outcroppings that lie within view of Denver's skyline and some of the area's most exquisite acreage. The short risk/reward, par-4 seventh, which lies on the west side of Ravenna's hog backs, is a great example of the breathtaking scenery you will experience.

It is the seventh, around which nature rises up in the form of pile after pile of rock that has a distinctly tortured look. Directly in front of the tee is a patch of ground rugged enough to be a wildlife preserve.

Beyond all the stone and its accompanying natural vegetation is the ultimate in manicured grass, along with a few bunkers. The contrast between the modern-day landscape techniques and the ages old geologic formations makes for grand scene.

The hole doglegs to the right and, as most short par 4s do, it gives the player two clear options.

If the direct route to the flagstick is taken from the back tee, it is only one giant stride more than 300 yards to the center of the green. But if that path is chosen, the ball must travel over the rocks, underbrush, a few trees and a couple of bunkers, one of which lies 15 yards short of the green.

The much more benign path requires a fairly straightforward drive out to the corner of the dogleg, although some of the rocky hazard must be carried to reach safety. A not-so-long approach is then called in order to gain access to a large putting surface.

A ridge runs across the green and a ball that winds up on the wrong side of the hump could result in a 75-foot putt that has to travel up and down to the cup.

Beyond the seventh holes lies more of the stony hillsides that were difficult to negotiate when settlers first came to the land, but which now provide character for those seeking a 21st-century homestead.

RED ROCKS

Country Club

16TH HOLE

355 yards • par 4

Morrison, Colorado 303•697•4438 www.redrockscountryclub.org

Photograph by Gary Caskey

One of Colorado's most distinctive locales is Red Rocks Park, where sandstone boulders millions of years old leave visitors in awe.

The park has its just place on the National Register of Historic Places and provides visual entertainment not found just anywhere.

A short distance up the road, with the rocks still very much in abundance, is an entertainment opportunity of another sort.

The Red Rocks Country Club evolved during the second half of the 20th century into a family-oriented gathering place. As one would expect, it features a golf course that takes full advantage of the natural wonders that leap out of the ground.

The largest of the rocks on the course, although by no means the largest in the area, looms behind the 16th green.

A gentle dogleg to the right, the par-4 16th presents no major ordeal off the tee. The ground rises slightly from the tee box out to the landing area and then moves sharply uphill to the green. At least one more club, or possibly two, will be needed than would be usual for the yardage left for the second shot.

With the ground climbing all the way to the green, and with a bunker protecting the right front, the approach shot is 100 percent carry.

And although it is certainly not in play, the giant slab of sandstone behind the green dominates the view.

Grooves etched in the rock, both horizontally and vertically, bring joy to geologists. The changing colors, depending on the angle of the sun, bring delight to the golfers.

A sizeable hill behind and to the right of the green also contains rocks that ooze out of the ground in various shapes and sizes. But they cannot compare with the big fellow that looks as if it might be a giant door to another kingdom.

The green itself is very shallow, adding to the difficulty of making the proper club selection from down in the fairway, and it slopes sharply from back to front.

There are just enough complexities to the hole to keep the golfer's mind from wandering. But the eyes never wander very far from the astonishing formation that towers overhead.

THE RIDGE

at Castle Pines North

18TH HOLE

390 yards • par 4

Castle Rock, Colorado 303•688•0100 www.theridgecpn.com

Photograph courtesy of Troon Golf

The Ridge at Castle Pines North—a Troon Golf-managed facility extolled as one of the best courses in the country on which the public can gain access—is filled with diversity.

The front side is fairly open, the back side is more enclosed. Length is an asset on the opening nine, there is a premium on accuracy coming home.

But when it comes to diversity, the 18th hole provides plenty enough all by its lonesome. It starts with potential turmoil, it ends with serenity.

Designer Tom Weiskopf won his only major championship at Royal Troon, and the ground on which he created this dazzling course bears absolutely no resemblance to the linksland on which he captured the British Open.

The view from the 18th tee at The Ridge is imposing at the very least. Rocks of all sizes and shapes lurch out of the ground to form a barrier that must be cleared simply to reach the ravine in front of them. And, of course, that ravine must also be cleared in order to reach the fairway.

The thought of having a ball strike one of the jagged hazards before sailing off at an unwanted angle toward deep vegetation will likely cause one to tee it up a little higher than usual.

Finding this fairway, therefore, is a very rewarding experience.

With all the rocks conquered, the player is left with a pleasant, slightly uphill view to a green perched behind two bunkers. The second shot needs to be carried all the way to the putting surface because in front of the green the grass is allowed to grow longer than fairway length.

The right-hand portion of the wide green is elevated, and a pin placement on that section is a three-putt invitation.

A final feast for the eyes is the ranchhouse-modern clubhouse that dominates the view directly behind the green. It is a refuge that brings about a far more calming atmosphere than did the view from the tee.

SANCTUARY

18TH HOLE

438 yards • par 4

Sedalia, Colorado 303•224•2860 www.sanctuarygolfcourse.com

Photograph by Dick Durrance II

With all the mountains available for viewing at Sanctuary, it is perhaps fitting that at the end of the day those playing the course have the opportunity to climb one.

Well, maybe not a real mountain. The elevation change is only about 60 feet, but that is still significant when trying to properly advance a golf ball.

There is vastness galore around Sanctuary, as is obvious from all the elevated tees that have been created by architect Jim Engh.

But Sanctuary's closing hole has something of a confining feel. It is situated in a valley with the ground sloping up on both sides of the fairway and the always-present pines dotting those slopes.

The assignment is clear from the tee. The ground rises up out of the valley to a ridge in the distance, and in two shots the player is expected to reach a green that is placed on a plateau about halfway up to that ridge.

It turns out to be something of a change of pace. After all, most of the round has been spent hitting downhill shots and then traveling uphill from the green to the next tee so that the senses can absorb yet another mountain view.

The tee shot at the 18th is only slightly uphill to a broad landing area with two bunkers on the left side of the fairway and the trees serving as a constant boundary.

The second shot is straight uphill. Or at least seems like it.

It is certainly all carry and even the accomplished players will find a mid-iron necessary to reach the crest of the relatively flat area where the green has been placed.

The green itself has two chief features. There is a false front on the right side, so any shot in that direction must carry well onto the green or face the possibility of rolling partway back down the hill.

In addition, the back third of the green falls away behind a ridge and creates a small area of putting surface where particularly difficult pin placements are available.

Having journeyed up the steep slope, it is once again possible to look back and see the mountains, a view that throughout a round at Sanctuary becomes commonplace.

At the end of the day, however, one comes to the easy conclusion that there is nothing commonplace about this golf course.

BALLYNEAL

8TH HOLE

515 yards • par 5

Holyoke, Colorado 970•854•5900 www.ballyneal.com

Photograph by Dick Durrance II

Ballyneal, an exquisite course designed by Tom Doak, is about a dozen miles from Nebraska and roughly 5,000 miles from Scotland.

One glance at the truly links-style course might make one guess that it was the other way around.

The sand hills that cover miles and miles in this relatively isolated area just cried out for a first-class golfing adventure, and Doak obliged.

"On this property, you will be isolated from others and yet see for miles," he said. "You will be lost in the vastness of the landscape and yet completely exposed to the elements."

Not only does the course look like it might have been imported from Scotland, it plays like the courses that line the coastlines of that country. The ground is firm and fast, and the wind takes only the occasional day off.

Five-time British Open champion Tom Watson has always professed that true golf should be played along the ground instead of through the air, and Ballyneal embraces that concept.

"The player who can control the flight of the ball," Doak said, "and who has the imagination to use the force of the wind and the contours of the ground to stop the ball where desired—in Scottish terms, the player who knows how to play real golf—will usually prevail."

Virtually any hole at Ballyneal could serve as an example of what the course is about, but the par-5 eighth will do nicely.

The fairway tumbles down a slope and then opens into a broad plain filled with humps and bumps and swales and dales. The lumpy nature of the ground is unceasing all the way to the green, although there is a mound with thick grass located just short and to the right of the putting surface.

The fairway blends right in with the green, which has four distinct hollows that create dramatically breaking putts. There is a bunker beyond the green, set into another rough-and-tumble mound.

When traveling to the region where golf was born and remains very much revered, it is best to be prepared for a different sort of game. The same can be said for Ballyneal.

THE GOLF CLUB AT BEAR DANCE

Photographs by Julie Gibson

18TH HOLE

655 yards • par 5

Larkspur, Colorado 303•681•4653 www.beardancegolf.com

The closing hole at The Golf Club at Bear Dance does not really span two zip codes. Or two counties. Or two ecosystems.

It just seems that way.

The 18th hole does stretch almost four-tenths of a mile through trees and around bunkers, and it provides a very big ending to a very big golf course.

Even from the tees used by those with medium to high handicaps, this hole extends to almost 600 yards and it settles for nothing less than shots that travel to the full measure of the club.

The tee shot is formidable enough by itself because it is pinched in by two rows of pines that direct the player out onto the distant, tumbling fairway.

There are few experiences in golf that can rival the sight of a ball traveling at a lofty trajectory between stands of trees and arriving safely on the far away short grass. The trouble with the 18th at Bear Dance is that such a shot is simply the start.

Once on the fairway, a right-to-left second shot is called for to accommodate the fact that the fairway turns that way and because there are two bunkers on the outside corner of the dogleg.

The second shot needs to come up short of three cross bunkers that are placed a little less than 100 yards from the green, but since those bunkers are about 555 yards from the tee, staying short of them is not much of a concern.

The main problem is just getting far enough down the fairway in two to be able to reach the green in regulation. The green is of the smallish variety with a deep bunker strategically placed on the front right of the putting surface, making the approach shot critical. There is also a grass swale behind the putting surface and getting up and down from that low spot is very problematic.

In keeping with the theme of naming each hole for a famous golfer, the 18th at Bear Dance honors Arnold Palmer. It is known as "The King," who even in his prime would have been quite happy to have walked away with a par on this king-sized hole.

THE BROADMOOR

18TH HOLE
Mountain Course

603 yards • par 5

Colorado Springs, Colorado 719•577•5887 www.broadmoor.com

Photograph by Dick Durrance II

When The Broadmoor wanted to refurbish what was originally known as its South Course, there was only one logical direction in which to turn.

Jack Nicklaus, after all, won his first U.S. Amateur title at the famous resort's East Course in 1959. So more than 45 years later he returned to put some punch into the newest of The Broadmoor's three courses.

It is now known as the Mountain Course, and it spreads out across the countryside on a majestic scale.

For those who want to put their game to the big test, the course can play as long as 7,700 yards. If one wishes a somewhat less imposing day of golf, there are plenty of tees to choose from along with the spacious fairways typically found on a Nicklaus layout.

The course comes to a close with a high-quality par 5 that moves up and down and all around the foothills. At 603 yards from the back tee, it forces even the longest of the long hitters to treat it as a three-shot hole.

There is a small bit of tall, thick prairie grass that must be carried with the tee shot, and more of the same is found down both sides of the fairway, creating trouble spots that must be avoided at all costs.

But between the problem areas there is an enormous expanse of short grass on which to place the tee shot.

The fairway makes a slight turn to the right for the second shot with the chief goal being to place the ball on a flat piece of ground about 70 to 90 yards from the green.

A left-hand turn is then made for the third shot, which is distinctly uphill to a complex green protected by a bunker on the front right. The green is multi-tiered with the back portion of the surface falling away into a shallow bowl.

The entire hole runs along the base of a dramatically rising hillside and part of the way up that hill is perched one of The Broadmoor's landmarks.

It is the Will Rogers Shrine, a monument built in memory of the legendary humorist by his good friend—Broadmoor founder Spencer Penrose.

Every 15 minutes chimes drift from the shrine down through the valley, sounding just as they did when Nicklaus made his first, triumphant trip to the property almost a half century ago.

CHERRY CREEK

Country Club

2ND HOLE

566 yards • par 5

Denver, Colorado 303•597•0300 www.cherrycreekcountryclub.com

Photograph by Ken May, Rolling Greens Photography

If there is no dramatic elevation change to work with or no huge rock outcropping or no pine forest, the great architect usually turns to strategy.

That's what the second hole at the Cherry Creek Country Club, sitting in the middle of a Denver neighborhood, is all about.

Jack Nicklaus has designed a thinking person's hole that features key bunkers and water in the form of an attractive little stream.

Just like on any par 5 that the big hitters hope to reach in two shots, those big hitters have two things on their to-do list. They want to hit it long, and they also want to hit it straight.

At Cherry Creek's second hole, the long shot will have a chance to get past the three bunkers that pinch in from the right and dramatically narrow the fairway. The straight shot will keep the ball between those bunkers and the creek that is a persistent nuisance down the left side.

Those capable of pounding the ball in the 300-yard plus range then will have a chance to reach the smallest green on the course, although the creek turns across the front of the putting surface and eventually must be dealt with no matter how many shots it takes to advance the ball down the fairway.

The normal course of action will be to leave the tee shot short of the fairway bunkers and well wide of the stream, after which a second shot can be directed toward a suitable layup yardage.

Staying to the right side of the fairway is the preferred path with the second shot since there is no need to flirt with the water as it makes its way up the left side.

The green and the area around it make up a picturesque complex of problems that need to be factored into the approach shot.

The creek runs at an angle across the face of the putting surface and beyond the creek to the left side of the green is a chipping area that can be a safe haven for those who have left themselves with a longer third shot than anticipated.

There is also a bunker to the left of the green and another just beyond it, plus another well-manicured chipping area over the green. Finally, the creek winds all the way around the putting surface and runs behind it, so an approach shot with too much zip on it can bound into the water.

It is never wise to lose one's focus while playing a Nicklaus course, and that is especially the case at Cherry Creek's second.

FOSSIL TRACE

Golf Club

12TH HOLE

585 yards • par 5

Golden, Colorado 303•277•8750 www.fossiltrace.com

Above photograph by Jim Hajek, PGA
Facing page photograph by Proshots

Golf takes a decidedly prehistoric turn at Fossil Trace, where there is an opportunity to advance one's knowledge of paleontology while trying to make the occasional 10-foot putt.

This truly unique course was laid out where the dinosaurs roamed and plenty of evidence has been unearthed to prove it. In addition, the mining of clay was a thriving enterprise on the property more than a century ago and some remnants of that operation are scattered here and there—some of them very much in play.

It all makes for an out-of-the-ordinary golfing experience and it is highlighted at the par-5 12th, which sets a standard for distinctive distractions.

As with most of the holes at Fossil Trace where a driver is used off the tee, there is plenty of room to hit it at the 12th. There is a bunker along the right edge of the fairway that needs to be avoided, but in truth that is the least of the player's worries.

The real action begins with the second shot because a series of hazards appear that are, to say the least, unusual.

At various intervals short of the green, rock formations rise up out of the otherwise pristine fairway like monoliths, and they must be circumvented in order to reach the putting surface.

The green itself sits between giant rock walls that loom like unconquerable fortresses. The biggest of the walls is behind and to the left of the green and an old mining steam shovel sits high atop the rock formation as a quaint reminder of the activities that once took place here.

And behind the rock wall there are fossils on display along with some footprints of those massive creatures that roamed the region millions of years ago.

As an added feature, parked on the front edge of the green is a nasty bunker that sits down in some grass mounds.

All in all, it is a hole that presents visual intimidation of the first order as well as a brief science lesson—a combination that in the world of golf is not found just anywhere.

FOX

FOX ACRES

Country Club

17TH HOLE

495 yards • par 5

Red Feather Lakes, Colorado 970•881•2191 www.foxacres.com

Photograph by Dick Durrance II

Golf is played in all manner of environments, but it thrives best where there is a level of solitude and serenity.

That means it thrives like crazy at Fox Acres.

When the opening hole of a golf course carries the name "Moose Crossing," we should be aware that the setting is right for a tranquil experience where nature is at the forefront and hubbub has been sent packing.

The country club community north and west of Fort Collins is nothing short of a mountain retreat in which the trees close in to create a feeling of isolation—especially on the golf course.

The trees that create that feeling are the key ingredient to the 17th hole, a par 5 on which preciseness is a more preferred trait than brute strength.

This hole is known as "Black Bear," and it is, indeed, a bear of a hole if the ball is not hit along the preferred path.

From the tee, it becomes immediately evident that a slight left-to-right action would be nice to have in the arsenal.

The forest encroaches on both sides of the fairway, but there are individual trees down the right side that especially come into play. A straight ball that barely eludes the trees on the right will be fine, but for safety's sake it is ideal to take the ball down the left side with a bit of right-handed fade.

Long hitters can reach for the green in two with relative ease, but the margin for error is small—due in part to a series of sentinel pines on the left that can swat down a shot heading in their direction.

The second shot is downhill, which reduces the yardage a bit, but just in front of the green is a deep swale, from which a pitch to the putting surface is blind.

That means a layup with the second shot is best left short of the swale so that a reasonably full shot can be lofted onto a green that has a ridge running across its mid-section.

Two bunkers on the front corners and two more on either side of the green compound the difficulty of the approach.

It is a thinking person's hole from start to finish, which is just fine since there is enough peace and quiet around to allow for a good think.

HARMONY CLUB

14TH HOLE

618 yards • par 5

Timnath, Colorado 970•224•4622 www.harmonyclub.info

Photograph by Dick Durrance II

The golfing phrase "risk-reward" does not mean the same thing to everyone.

Those who hit the ball an average length consider the opportunity for risk taking to be the reward other people get when they blast a tee shot 300 yards.

For the big hitters, the reward comes when that 300-yard shot is followed by a risk successfully taken.

However it is viewed, the risks and rewards come into play at Harmony Club's par-5 14th—one of the fascinating adventures found on a very recent addition to Colorado's list of golfing treasures.

Like all good risk-reward holes, this one can be tamed even by those not supremely gifted. Three steady shots, none needing to be massive, create the likelihood of a par and the possibility of a birdie.

But those with a taste for greatness, and the length off the tee to match, can attempt something special.

The tee shot looks more ominous than it really is. There are, indeed, trees and a creek down the left side and a lot of undulation to the ground on the right. The fairway, however, is fairly wide so the chief problem off the tee is to free the mind of the potential problems and make a smooth swing.

Once on the short grass, it is decision time. For most, that decision is easy. One simply advances the ball down the fairway, perhaps with an iron, past the wetlands area on the left and beyond a nest of cottonwood trees.

Having achieved that task, the player turns left and lofts a short third shot over the creek that has traveled the length of the hole. A bunkerless green awaits in the midst of rolling landscape.

For those who wish, however, the risk is there to take. After a big tee shot, a shortcut can be taken directly over the wetlands that fill the inside corner of the dogleg.

Cutting across means a second shot might need to carry "only" about 210 to 240 yards.

But if the effort comes up short or sails left, the ball plops down into the marshy grass. If it drifts right, it slams into the creek—which is fairly deep and is lined by tall grass and the cottonwoods.

Plenty of character is added along the way by the ground tumbling like waves in a green ocean. It is a hole that when safely negotiated can provide a distinct golfing reward—whether or not it involves a risk.

MARIANA BUTTE

Golf Course

16TH HOLE

561 yards • par 5

Loveland, Colorado 970•667•8308 www.golfloveland.com

Photographs by Lee Kline Photographics

Carved out of the foothills west of Loveland and only an hour's drive north from downtown Denver, the Mariana Butte Golf Course has firmly established itself as a favorite destination of golfers everywhere. Mariana is a four-and-a-half star-rated, premier course featuring three distinct characteristics. The front nine winds its way through a lush creek bottom meadow where Dry Creek, which is anything but, crisscrosses numerous holes. The back nine begins with holes that play in and out of rock outcroppings that boast elevated tees and stunning views of the nearby Rocky Mountains. Golfers finish their round by navigating holes that tuck in along the Big Thompson River and play back up to Mariana's Butte for which the course was named.

Dick Phelps was given the go-ahead to design and create a layout that featured spectacular holes that were both interesting and challenging and ones that golfers would remember and want to play again and again. He took that concept and everything Mother Nature had to offer and created just such a place in Mariana Butte's 16th hole.

Standing on the back tee of No. 16, players get a feel for why it is named "Wompawara" after a Kiowa chief. Translated it means "He who scares all men." Just how intimidating the hole might be depends on the skill level of the player, but even the most talented golfer will have cause for concern upon reaching the tee and will need to rely on their best ball placement expertise.

There is an abundance of picturesque predicaments to address along this double-dogleg hole. From the back tee, the Big Thompson River curves in front of the tee and stretches right along the intended flight path for the drive. Eventually, however, the river gives way to Dry Creek and tall, mature cottonwoods that guard the fairway on both sides as obstacles to wayward drives.

Golfers have a 205-yard carry to clear both the Big Thompson and a portion of the creek that intersects the fairway at a strategic point, creating a hazard for those who hope to clear it. Better make your first shot count; too tight right or too tight left spells trouble.

After a safe tee shot, next on the card is to avoid the lake on the left side of the fairway up near the green. A second shot precisely placed to the right of the water and golfers are in position for an approach shot into a green protected on two sides by bunkers. That is if you stay focused.

With water, trees, more water, and sand all playing a prominent role, Mariana Butte's 16th is worthy of having a tee named after someone who was thought to be synonymous with fear.

OMNI INTERLOCKEN

Resort Golf Club

4TH HOLE
Vista Nine

Photographs courtesy of Omni Interlocken Resort Golf Club

565 yards • par 5

Broomfield, Colorado 303•438•6600 www.omnihotels.com

Although they often get taken for granted, the views on a Colorado golf course are nevertheless spectacular as long as one can find the high ground.

Finding the high ground at the Omni Interlocken Resort turns out to be as easy as reading the names of the three nine-hole courses on the property.

Since one of those courses is referred to as the Vista Nine, that seems like the ideal place to start. And the hole that delivers the best vista of all is the par-5 fourth, which, sure enough, sits on the highest point of all.

Actually, it is the green that is at Omni Interlocken's pinnacle and to get there a player must climb 68 feet from the tee on a hole that is long enough to begin with and obviously plays longer than the listed yardage.

The fourth on the Vista Nine is a perfect kind of hole for a resort course in that it hides no secrets. Those who are playing it for the first time can tell what it is all about at a glance.

Two straight, solid shots are needed to set up the approach to the green. Straight is required because there is a property boundary to the left of the fairway, and solid is desired even more than usual because the uphill nature of the landscape does not allow for much roll.

A pair of bunkers on the left side of the fairway 150 yards from the green impedes the second shot, and another bunker guards the right-front section of the putting surface. The rest of the green blends in neatly with the fairway, creating the opportunity for a straightforward chip and a par-saving putt.

Once on the green, the Denver skyline is visible. So are the Flatirons of Boulder. So is Pikes Peak, 75 miles away. Familiar scenes, all, but still impressive when viewed from a distance as well as when viewed after recording a good score on a long, uphill par 5.

THE CLUB AT PRADERA

Photographs by Jim Engh

7TH HOLE

594 yards • par 5

Parker, Colorado 303•607•5700 www.theclubatpradera.com

Although many an attempt has been made, it is truly difficult to replicate the kind of golfing experience one finds in Ireland.

The Club at Pradera comes about as close as possible.

Architect Jim Engh refers to it as a "modern-Irish-Colorado" course. That is an apt description for a layout placed amid the rolling landscape south and west of Denver that now is home to a host of nationally recognized designs.

"There are many holes where we're basically leaving the land as we found it," Engh said. "We sculpted a few features into this terrain and then left the rest natural. We worked hard to blend what nature gave us and what we fine-tuned."

The combination of modern and Irish is on full display at the par-5 seventh. It is target golf placed in a setting laced with undergrowth and natural grasses.

It is possible to play the hole relatively safe, with three tidy shots reasonably assuring a par, or to play it dangerously with the lure being a tap-in birdie or perhaps an eagle. The risky way, naturally, also creates the possibility of a score that unpleasantly inflates the 18-hole total.

From any of the tees embedded in a hillside, the safe shot carries into the left of the two fairways and short of two bunkers that pinch in and leave only a wisp of a fairway through which to walk.

The second shot travels along the same line to a wide landing area. From there, the player makes a right-hand turn and pitches the ball toward a green surrounded by bushes and grasses that create a natural hazard. There is a false front on the green and deep bunkers both short and long.

And then there is the dangerous path. In one big blast, a drive can be aimed at a smaller fairway to the right of the safe landing zone. It is an island in the midst of all the rugged nature and it sits beyond a ridge on which two bunkers are located. From that patch of fairway, it is a short distance to the green and the hoped-for birdie.

A player can be safe, sorry or satisfied at Pradera's seventh, which as one thinks about it is pretty much what golf is all about.

THE GOLF CLUB AT RAVENNA

14TH HOLE

612 yards • par 5

Denver, Colorado 720•956•1600 www.ravennagolf.com

Photograph by Ken May, Rolling Greens Photography

With golf balls going farther than they once did and with drivers getting bigger and bigger, the course designers of the world have responded by building holes that cover more and more yardage.

Those who do not hit the ball into the adjacent county are perfectly free to choose a set of tees to suit their own game, but if a player wants to be tested to the fullest, newer courses have made that test more robust.

At the Jay Morrish-designed Ravenna layout, a sumptuous new course set in rugged surroundings, there are tests all over the place. Particularly at the par-5 14th.

It is not unusual in today's golfing world to find a par 5 as long as Ravenna's 14th, but there are no shortcuts on this hole. The 612 yards listed on the scorecard are very earnest yards.

The hole is slightly downhill, but not dramatically so. There are no doglegs to cut across. It's just a substantial hole on which the full measure of the clubs selected need to be extracted.

The 14th is one of the narrowest driving holes on the course with a water hazard running down the left side and rough that falls off into a native area on the right.

The creek to the left of the fairway eventually makes a right turn and forms a pond that runs all the way to the front edge of the green. To the left of the pond is an area of safety that the long hitters might choose to reach in two. The typical second shot layup needs to come to rest short of the pond, leaving a short iron over the water to a green guarded by a back left bunker.

Ravenna and its surroundings are designed with modern creature comforts very much in mind so that an escape from the all-out pace of life can be realized as much as possible.

And Ravenna also has the kind of challenges to test those with the ability to skillfully employ today's high-tech golfing equipment.

RED ROCKS

Country Club

18TH HOLE

526 yards • par 5

Morrison, Colorado 303•697•4438 www.redrockscountryclub.org

Photograph by Tom Pidgeon

At the conclusion of 17 holes of golf at the Red Rocks Country Club, a treat awaits.

What is seen from the 18th tee is, in a word, panoramic—which is defined as an unobstructed view over a wide area.

There are rugged hills not all that far away. There are mountains farther in the distance. There is the natural splendor of the sandstone outcroppings that give the landscape such a unique look and also give the course its name.

Also visible are the dwellings of those who have sought out a place of uncommon beauty in which to live.

And right over there is the stunning Red Rocks Amphitheater, one of the most unique concert halls in the world where artists perform on a stage carved out of stone.

Finally, there is the par-5 18th hole—one that gives the player a chance for a memorable conclusion to the day's activity.

If such a broad view is available, it stands to reason the last hole at Red Rocks is downhill. And the landing area is, indeed, about 70 feet below the tee.

A small grove of cottonwoods and pines guards the right side of the fairway and to the left there is a cluster of three bunkers built into a mound. On the edge of the first bunker is a chunk of rock, a reminder of the much larger versions scattered around the nearby countryside.

The chief feature of the hole, however, is the manner in which the ground moves. The fairway drifts down and down and down from the tee and then, about 240 yards from the green, starts up again.

That means the tee shot is virtually certain to finish on a slope—usually leaving a downhill, sidehill lie that forces a certain amount of skill to come into play for the second shot.

Those who lay up with their second need to avoid the bunkers short of the green and then, with the third shot, two other bunkers to the right of the putting surface provide potential problems.

Because the 18th is not massive in length, there is every reason to expect a good score on a hole that not only brings the round to a close, but which affords the textbook definition of a panorama.

SANCTUARY

1 ST HOLE

604 yards • par 5

Sedalia, Colorado 303•224•2860 www.sanctuarygolfcourse.com

Photograph by Dick Durrance II

Since most golf courses are considered sanctuaries of a sort, it takes a pretty special place to call itself Sanctuary with a capital "S."

Such a special place exists south of Denver. It takes up 222 acres surrounded by over 12,000 acres of dedicated open space and is nothing short of a preserve. Only 9,000 rounds are permitted a year—about 40 percent of them coming in charity tournaments that typically raise $5 million per season.

The goal at this haven is to provide a refuge for all living things, including those with four feet, those who take wing, those that slither along the ground, and those that emerge out of the soil and grow to great heights.

Golfers, too, are treated to a locale tailored for their endeavors, which becomes evident from the vista available on the very first tee. It is about 200 feet from the so-called Rattlesnake Tee down to the landing area, and the fairway slopes about 80 more feet from there down to the green.

So even though the hole measures at just over 600 yards, the big hitters can still reach the green in two.

Like most of the holes on the course, and so many others in the state, the first at Sanctuary is as much a work of art as it is a playing field, one surrounded by pines that stand with proper military bearing.

The first major obstacle is a bunker on the right side of the fairway. It is listed as being 290 yards from the tee but plays more like 220. The average player will stay short of the trap in a fairly wide part of the fairway, but the long hitter will try to get past the bunker into a narrow landing area.

The most significant feature of the hole, however, is found short and right of the green in the form of a large bowl—at the bottom of which is a pond. The safe play is to stay short of the bowl and then pitch over it to the hourglass-shaped green beyond.

Those going for it in two have the ultimate risk-reward shot facing them, one that is very much a no-nonsense affair. That, however, should come as no surprise because as one soon discovers at Sanctuary, the environment, the scenery, the contributions to charity and the golf are all serious business.

CHAPTER TWO

Red Sky Ranch & Golf Club 12th Hole, Norman Course

The Club at Crested Butte 11th Hole

Aspen Glen Golf Club 6th Hole

ASPEN GLEN

Golf Club

8TH HOLE

162 yards • par 3

Carbondale, Colorado 970•704•1988 www.aspen-glen.com

Photograph by Dick Durrance II

The 18 holes at Aspen Glen, as is the case at many courses, have each been given names of their own.

And there is no reason to argue with the name that has been given to the par-3 eighth on the dramatic course put together by two generations of the Nicklaus family.

The hole is called River's Edge for obvious reasons since the Roaring Fork River flows alongside at a brisk pace.

But it is possible no one would have complained had the hole, instead, been referred to as Razor's Edge. There is, after all, a very fine line between success and failure on a hole that takes full advantage of the glorious surroundings.

Sitting off in the distance, just to the left of the flight path to the green, is Mount Sopris. It falls just short of being included in Colorado's renowned 14,000-foot peaks, but not by much. And with the Roaring Fork moving along to the left of the hole, plus the rocks that line the river and the occasional boulder that pops up for added visual appeal, the eighth hole is something special to see.

But there is also golf to be played, and at the eighth, that turns out to be special as well.

The tee shot is all carry with the ball having to travel over a little rough and a lot of bunker that sprawls across the very front of the green.

There is a front level and a back level to the green, and if too much club has been used the back bunker can easily come into play.

Most of all, however, the tee shot must not be allowed to stray to the left. A smallish bunker has been placed just left of the green, and to the left of the bunker the ground falls away sharply down to the rocks and the water.

That is where the "Razor's Edge" thought comes into the picture. If the ball lands in a particular spot alongside the green, there is a chance for a chip and a par-saving putt. But just a few inches to the left of that particular spot, the ball will almost certainly bound down into the hazard.

It is a hole with glorious attractions built on the edge of danger, and it is up to the player to enjoy the former while avoiding the latter.

CATAMOUNT

Ranch & Club

8TH HOLE

211 yards • par 3

Steamboat Springs, Colorado 970•871•9200 www.catamountranchclub.com

Photograph by David Thiemann

From a visual standpoint, there is something of just about everything at the Catamount Ranch & Club, and all of it is remarkable.

The Tom Weiskopf-designed course starts out in ranchland, travels through the aspens and then, on the back nine, climbs 400 feet to a high point at the 16th tee amid the kind of high country scenery that is synonymous with the area around Steamboat Springs.

"We started with a working ranch in a spectacular setting and created a course of uncommon distinction," Weiskopf said in describing yet another of his unique endeavors.

"Because of the elevation changes, mountain courses pose special challenges. But once you overcome those challenges, the beauty and the views can be dramatic."

Weiskopf is not fond of the phrase "signature hole," and because of that there is no such designation attached to his courses.

At Catamount Ranch, choosing a signature hole would have been close to impossible, anyway, because of the many possibilities.

One of those that might have been considered for such an honor would surely have been the par-3 eighth, which is equal parts imposing and entrancing.

It is an 80-foot drop from the back tee to the green, and the ball must travel over the dazzling, fast-moving waters of Walton Creek, which itself is surrounded by trees and undergrowth of seemingly limitless varieties.

On the other side of all the trouble is a green that presents its own difficulties, chief among them being the fact that it is hard to hit.

The green is wide, but quite shallow and angles away from the player. It is also protected across its broad front by a winding bunker that must be carried in order to reach every pin position except one placed on the very front-left corner.

Beyond the green are the high mountain meadows that make up much of the surrounding landscape and provide the canvas on which Weiskopf has composed a golfing mural.

THE CLUB AT CORDILLERA

7TH HOLE
The Summit Course

198 yards • par 3

Edwards, Colorado 970•926•5300 www.cordillera-vail.com
Photograph by Henebry Photography

When creating a mountain golf course, it often becomes evident that there is little need to move a lot of earth.

The earth on the slopes usually looks pretty good to begin with, and nobody wants to disrupt it any more than necessary.

In building The Summit Course at The Club at Cordillera, Jack Nicklaus thought he would need to displace about 600 tons of dirt. By the time the project was completed, less than 175 tons had been moved.

"We wanted to do as little as possible and use the trees and the environment to our advantage," he said.

Some ground was obviously rearranged in the building of the par-3 seventh, but only enough to sculpt the tees and a green that is stately in appearance.

A stand of long, wispy grass—that tends to take on a golden color—crosses the player's path between the tee and the green at the seventh. Low-growing shrubs surround the hole, and the ever-present aspens serve as a backdrop.

The green itself rests on a mini-plateau, and the best advice from the tee is do not miss it to the right. A shot hit in that direction will likely find the bottom of a king-sized bunker that will not only engulf the ball but the golfer as well.

A false front has been placed on the green, and a shot landing there will run off the putting surface. Other bunkers are found on the left front and just over the back left.

Between those two traps the ground rises, but only slightly. That provides something of a safe area from which a par might be saved. Missing the green to the left is far superior to missing it to the right.

Nicklaus may not have moved a lot of ground in building The Summit Course, but when he did, as is evident with the seventh hole, he left something special.

THE CLUB AT CRESTED BUTTE

7TH HOLE

210 yards • par 3

Crested Butte, Colorado 970•349•6131 www.theclubatcrestedbutte.com

Photograph by Tom Stillo

The old mining town of Crested Butte, which prides itself on maintaining its neighborly attitude, many years ago became a forerunner in the world of high mountain golf.

Sitting at the base of pine-covered slopes in a valley created by the Slate River, the Club at Crested Butte was designed by Robert Trent Jones II and provides all the gorgeous sights and all the pulse-quickening tests one would expect on a course that sits 9,000 feet above sea level.

The river is often visible during the course of play, and so is the town itself, which was built in the 1880s to serve as a hub for miners and ranchers and now finds itself a lure for tourists looking for a slower pace of life. That reduced pace has caused more and more of those visitors to become residents.

Towering above everything are the various peaks, and they gaze down on a course that has an especially fascinating assortment of par 3s.

One of those is the seventh, which gives the player very clear options. If safety is considered the prudent play, there is plenty of room available in which to be safe. But if boldness is the order of the day, nothing but a crisp shot struck with the proper club will do.

The target is very wide and not all that deep and, as is often the case with holes of this type of design, there is a bunker placed behind the green in order to collect balls that have been given a little boost.

There is reason to give the tee shot a little boost, of course. It comes in the form of a lake that runs across almost the entire front of the green. And far more often than not the pin is placed on the left portion of the green, so that the water must be carried if anything resembling a birdie putt is the goal.

Out to the right, however, is an abundance of short grass that invites those faint of heart. After all, it is still possible to make par from there. But if the hole has been cut to the extreme left of the green, a very long chip shot awaits those who have purposely stayed away from the water.

Most good holes give players a choice, and this long par 3 spells out those choices in the clearest golfing language possible.

THE CLUB AT CRESTED BUTTE

11TH HOLE

177 yards • par 3

Crested Butte, Colorado 970•349•6131 www.theclubatcrestedbutte.com

Photograph by Tom Stillo

At some point during the course of a round, there occurs a moment when the player realizes he or she is being called upon to strike what needs to be the best shot of the day. Or something close to it.

That moment should not come early on. A thoughtful architect allows a player to get into the round a little bit so that the swing can find something resembling a groove and the tension can be allowed to ease.

And then, suddenly, the bell sounds. The time arrives when quality has to make a showing or else there is a price to pay.

At The Club at Crested Butte, that moment comes on the 11th tee. By now, the pulse has hopefully dwindled and the first-time visitor has become accustomed to the magnificence of the surroundings.

So it is a perfect time to take a breath and hit a golf shot of which one can be proud.

The medium-long par 3 offers virtually no room for error. A shot to the left of the green might find a grassy haven, but even that is problematic. There is really no choice but to aim at the middle of the green and fire away.

It is a slightly downhill tee shot and it must carry a pond that inches its way almost to the front edge of the green.

Because of the all-or-nothing nature of the shot, the green has a reasonable amount of depth to it, especially in its midsection. There are bunkers behind the green, however, meaning that it is not wise to simply take one extra club and bang away in hopes of taking the water completely out of play.

The ground behind the green rises up into a mound, helping give the hole an amphitheater look from the tee. And all around there are the mountains coated with the pines and aspen, not to mention the occasional four-legged or winged creatures that might stroll or fly into view.

For a brief moment, however, all of that needs to be put aside at the 11th tee so that contemplation can turn to the task of hitting what one hopes will be the best shot of the day.

HAYMAKER

Golf Course

12TH HOLE

163 yards • par 3

Steamboat Springs, Colorado 970•870•1846 www.haymakergolf.com

Photographs by Dave Thiemann

There had been other attempts at building a golf course a few miles south of Steamboat Springs before Keith Foster came along.

Various piles of debris were actually lying around to attest to those failed ventures.

But that did not deter Foster, who has experience in bringing golf courses to life in unexpected places. He took an ugly, abandoned rock quarry smack dab in the middle of San Antonio, Texas and turned it into one of the most fascinating places to play golf anywhere in the land.

Give him a lovely chunk of high mountain ranchland and it figured he could crank out a course that would act as a magnet during the months when snow is not on the ground.

Presto, the Yampa Valley suddenly was home to the municipally owned Haymaker course. It has been recognized as an Audubon Signature Course, meaning it is as environmentally friendly as they come. A gathering of blue heron has even set up shop on the grounds.

Conservation is a lifestyle cornerstone in this part of the world, and the Haymaker has disturbed only 110 of the course's 233 acres for the tees, fairways and greens. The rest of the rolling grassland, of which there is an abundance, has been left alone.

Part of the altered 110 acres has become the 12th hole, which brings the kind of golf played elsewhere in the country to a Colorado setting. There is so much natural wonder in the state that players do not often see the sort of hole one might find in Florida, say, or the desert.

Haymaker's par-3 12th is just that. It calls for either an all-out carry over a small lake in order to reach the middle or the right portion of the green or a shot to the left edge of the putting surface, thus allowing a player to avoid having to traverse the water. A strip of fairway runs along the left bank of the lake and serves as a bail-out area for the less adventurous.

Other than the water, the player sees two landmarks from the tee. One is a mound behind the right side green with a grouping of sand and grass bunkers burrowing into it.

There is also a short, stone wall separating the water from the green which does something every major design feature should do—separate a good shot from a bad one.

KEYSTONE RANCH

5TH HOLE

190 yards • par 3

Keystone, Colorado 800•464•3494 www.golfkeystone.com

Photograph by Ken Redding

Island greens have become quite commonplace from Florida to California, so it should not be too surprising to find one located on a mountain course in Colorado.

It is, however, not the average island green.

Keystone Ranch Golf Course, designed by Robert Trent Jones Jr., works its way through high pastures with lodgepole pines all around. A nine-acre lake even comes into play, although that lake is not what encompasses the island green.

Instead, the design feature in question appears on a hole with no water on it at all, the par-3 fifth.

The fifth is laid out in a classic mountain meadow, one abundant with thick, hearty grass. Hills surround the scene, higher in some places than others, with pines filling the sides of the slopes.

There are even some weathered barns behind the green to remind all who pass of days gone by.

In the midst of all this is the green, and what makes it an island is the fact that, to get to it, the ball must carry the natural grasses, which will inhale a golf ball to the point that it might be difficult and maybe impossible to locate.

The green is quite wide and much deeper on the right side than on the left. Unlike most island greens, however, there are some areas of safe haven to be found other than just on the putting surface.

Several yards of "prepared" grass have been created short of the green, so a tee shot that comes up just a little short can still find relative safety. There is also a small bunker in front of the green, a larger one to the right and another big one at the back left.

When taking in the view from the fifth tee, the word "rustic" springs to mind. It is a view that has been unchanged for a very long time except for the fact that now there is a small island of green in the middle of it.

THE RIVER COURSE

at Keystone

7TH HOLE

195 yards • par 3

Keystone, Colorado 800•464•3494 www.golfkeystone.com

Above photograph by Leisa Gibson
Facing page photograph by Ken May

As one would suspect from its name, The River Course at Keystone has a river running through it. And it is just not any old stream.

The Snake River becomes a significant hazard on the front nine of a course designed by Michael Hurdzan and Dana Fry, who have projects scattered not only around the country but around the world.

"Our philosophy is to design golf courses that stir the spirit, exceed expectation and defy understanding," Hurdzan said.

"In doing this, golf becomes a complex puzzle requiring strength, skill and strategy—set in an environment of unquestioning beauty yet subject to the irrepressible forces of nature."

That's quite a lofty goal, but the ground with which Hurdzan and Fry had to work at The River Course allowed them to reach it.

The crown jewel is the seventh, a par 3 at which the Snake River plays a prominent role. Each hole at The River Course bears a name, and the seventh is called, quite simply, "Snake."

Surrounding the various tees is the natural growth—profuse and luxuriant grasses that grow right down to the riverside.

The river itself is not enormous, but it is certainly wide enough to be called a river. In the bed, peeking above the water, are stones that are sized somewhere between rocks and boulders. And it is entirely likely that the sun will be reflecting off the water to give the viewer an image fitting of a high-budget cinema.

It is, as Hurdzan suggests, an environment of unquestioning beauty.

There is another small strip of undergrowth on the other side of the river, after which the work of the architect takes hold in the form of fairway-length grass leading up to a green that rises to a crown and then falls away for a total depth of 39 yards.

The green is only 24 yards wide and is protected on either side by bunkers that are well below the level of the putting surface.

Hurdzan's suggestion that such a picture exceeds expectation and defies understanding is very poetic, but the spectacular clearly becomes very much expected in this part of the world. Anyone who plays it, however, would likely agree that the seventh at The River Course stirs the spirit.

LAKOTA CANYON RANCH

Golf Club

17TH HOLE

198 yards • par 3

New Castle, Colorado 970•984•9700 www.lakotacanyonranch.com

Photograph by Dick Durrance II

For players with a fair amount of skill, there is not much reason for missing the 17th green at the Lakota Canyon Ranch Golf Club.

It looks to be, after all, about the size of a shopping mall parking lot—a massive 58 yards in length. True, the back third of the green is quite a bit narrower than the front portion and sits behind a ridge that creates two levels to the putting surface.

Nevertheless, it is a big target that needs to be hit in one stroke. Or else.

If the tee shot does not come to rest on the closely mown grass, chances are it will be at the bottom of a ravine, somewhere in a quite unpleasant bunker or on the side of one of the slopes that separate the green from the brush and lumpy ground that make up most of the property.

The hole plays downhill, which is the norm on golf courses where the scenery is a major attraction, and there is a miniature canyon between the tee and the green. Such a hazard usually puts a lump in the throat of the high handicapper, but those with a smooth swing and the proper follow-through will consider it to be a routine nuisance.

Indeed, by the time the players have reached the 17th hole at Lakota, they have surely grown used to dealing with the deep gashes in the ground.

The front of the oversized green runs almost to the very edge of the ravine. So taking the proper club from the tee is vital. In fact, there could be a four- or five-club difference depending on where the flagstick is positioned.

A lone bunker on the hole sits just to the right of the front portion of the green and is typical of the ones at Lakota—expansive.

The ground rises up around the back portion of the green, creating the slight opportunity for a ball to bounce off a slope and trickle in the direction of the hole.

Luck, however, should not be counted on at this hole. Instead, bringing along at least a bit of skill is recommended.

MAROON CREEK

Club

11TH HOLE

163 yards • par 3

Aspen, Colorado 970•920•1533

Photograph by Dick Durrance II

Praise be to the artist with the skill to adequately capture the aspen as it appears in autumn.

From lemony yellow to burnished bronze, the aspen tend to take your breath away when in full fall color. That is especially so on a golf course, where the works of nature always seem to become magnified.

At the 11th hole of the Maroon Creek Club, for instance, the aspen help create no less than a tapestry that all but overshadows the golf.

The course is, appropriately enough, about two miles from Aspen itself. It is the design work of Tom Fazio, who at the base of Buttermilk Mountain laid out the first four holes in a ranchland setting and then routed the layout through a canyon, across high meadows and along the banks of Maroon Creek.

Upon reaching the 11th tee, such matters as the hole location and what club to hit become somewhat secondary as the view is absorbed—particularly late in the golfing season when the stand of aspen behind the green has gone through its hue-altering process.

There is, however, more to this par 3 than just the trees.

It is dramatically downhill, for one thing. The green is about 85 feet below the level of the back tee, and the slope in front of the tee is filled with native vegetation.

The green is an island in the midst of thick grass, undergrowth and the trees, which lurk very near the playing field so that an incorrect club selection or improper trajectory can send the ball sailing into the forest.

A bunker is cut into the left side of the green, acting as a catcher's mitt for balls that might otherwise bound down a slope toward Maroon Creek. To the right, a ridge runs down from a hillside and right onto the green, forming a hump that, in turn, creates very awkward putts.

The 11th at Maroon Creek is clearly treacherous. But it is also among the state's many visual masterpieces thanks in no small measure to the always stunning aspen.

RED SKY

Ranch & Golf Club

2ND HOLE

Norman Course

200 yards • par 3

Wolcott, Colorado 866•873•3759 www.redskygolfclub.com

Photograph by Allen Kennedy

Just up the highway from Vail is a 700-acre complex that presents the sport of golf on what seems to be an almost limitless scale.

It is the Red Sky Ranch & Golf Club, which since its creation in 2002 has not only drawn accolades from various publications but which has been featured on a national television travel show as one of the leading "hidden gems" in all of the nation.

Those who dwell within its boundaries can take advantage of two dazzling courses designed by a couple of the most familiar names golf has to offer—Greg Norman and Tom Fazio.

Both courses wander across the hillsides, edge their way around ravines and rock outcroppings and generally crisscross through an awe-inspiring Colorado wilderness.

"For years, my love of the Rockies, along with the natural beauty of the surroundings, has beckoned me to the Vail Valley," Norman said when his course was opened. Architectural critics promptly called it his best work.

Very soon after embarking on the Norman Course, it becomes clear what the day's adventure will be all about.

From the tee at the par-3 second hole, the panorama is staggering. From the very back, the target is 200 yards away and there is a lot of green to shoot at. But the rugged nature of the landscape creeps right up to the spot where play begins.

Just to the left of the tee box are rocks, rough, small trees and all manner of unkempt but naturally beautiful surroundings. To the right of the tee is an area in which very tall people might disappear completely if they should unwisely choose to go exploring.

The ground falls and then rises again between the tee and green, and a bunker of massive proportion has been built into the slope in front of and all the way around the right side of the green. The putting surface itself is large enough to have its own zip code, so just because the ball has reached the green does not mean the golf is almost over.

The vast amount of splendor visible while playing the second hole makes the devoted player quite thrilled that the round is just beginning.

RED SKY

Ranch & Golf Club

17TH HOLE

Fazio Course

168 yards • par 3

Wolcott, Colorado 866•873•3759 www.redskygolfclub.com

Photograph by Allen Kennedy

Because of the enormous scale of the two golf courses at Red Sky Ranch, it is often the case that the hole being played at that particular moment is the only one that can be seen.

Everybody knows there are other holes all over the place, but they are hidden by the rises and falls in a very, very large piece of land.

Such is the situation at the next-to-last hole on the Tom Fazio course.

From the 17th tee, mountains are visible near and mountains are visible far. Close by are a few residences of sizable proportions. The scenery gives the impression of being the absolute end of the Earth if the end of the Earth happened to be in Colorado.

And right in the middle of this almost overpowering scene is a golf hole. It should come as no surprise that it is a very good looking one, at that.

It is a par 3 of medium length and is placed in something of a bowl surrounded by pines. There is even a pond, adding to the peaceful nature of the surroundings.

The tee on the 17th hole is located somewhat above the green, and the pond takes up space slightly to the left of the direct path down to the putting surface.

The target has something of a boomerang shape as it wraps around the water and the bunker, which has been squeezed in between the pond and the green. There is also a trap on the right side, and it gets quite a bit of action from those who want to make sure they stay out of the liquid hazard.

Because the green is so deep, proper club selection is paramount. That is especially true when the flagstick is located at the very back of the green, in which case it is also tucked behind the water.

The view from the 17th tee is almost boundless. But as so often happens at Red Sky Ranch, that view does not include any other hole on the golf course.

THE GOLF CLUB AT REDLANDS MESA

12TH HOLE

141 yards • par 3

Grand Junction, Colorado 866•863•9270 www.redlandsmesa.com

Photograph by Dick Durrance II

When it comes time to design the first golf course on the moon, Jim Engh will surely be among those consulted for the project.

There seems to be no piece of ground too exotic for him to create a visionary set of holes.

And after seeing some of Engh's more well-known works, his trademarks become fairly easy to spot. There they are once more at The Golf Club at Redlands Mesa, a course built on ground that is at the same time inhospitable and alluring.

No ordinary bunkers will be found on one of Engh's courses, and there will often be mounding around greens that stand out as symbolic of his designs. Both of these features are part of the Redlands Mesa's 12th hole, which was built in the midst of some of the area's typically rugged landscape.

As with many shots on this course, the one from the 12th tee is well within the average player's skill level. No massive blast is required to clear the native grasses and the rocks between the tee and green. Just a smooth strike with what will probably be only a short iron.

The green is also quite inviting because there is so much of it, covering a large distance from side to side to the point that three putts are commonplace. But it needs to be large in order to fit appropriately into the vastness of the surroundings.

Protecting the right-front portion of the green is one of those non-ordinary bunkers found on Engh's courses. This one starts out as a wide expanse well short of the green and then narrows as it nears the putting surface. And since the trap is well below the green, it takes an expert-like explosion shot for the player to have a realistic chance at saving par.

Behind the green is a wall of rock and rough ground that overshadows the tranquil turf on which the players are doing their best. Between the green and the rock, the earth rises to form a mound that gives an arena-like look to the entire scene.

For those familiar with his courses, the hole is unmistakable Engh. Which means it presents what is always a sought-after combination: It is fun to play, and it is stunning to look at.

RIO GRANDE

Club & Golf Course

14TH HOLE

Photographs by Ken May, Rolling Greens Photography

207 yards • par 3

South Fork, Colorado 719•873•1995 www.riograndeclub.com

It is common to find a par 3 on which the tee shot needs to stay in the air all the way to the green.

And on such holes the problem is usually spelled out in no uncertain terms. It might be a lake or it might be a ravine or it might be an acre of sand.

At the Rio Grande Club, however, there is a little bit of everything between the tee and the green at the par-3 14th—a delightfully attractive hole on which a variety of natural stumbling blocks stand ready to put a ball in peril.

The most obvious difficulty is all the native grass that grows tall enough so that it can wave in the wind. But weaving its way through the grass is a creek that heads up the length of the hole and then turns to the left just a little in front of the green.

There are rocks bordering the creek, adding to the overall rugged look of the hole, some of them of boulder dimensions. A ball that encounters one of the rocks might go anywhere.

An added attraction is the bunker that fits between the creek and the green, providing a final hurdle.

There is actually a bail-out area to the right of the green, and a shot aimed in that direction that comes up just a little short can also find a small portion of short grass adjacent to the creek. But the green is a lot bigger than the bail-out area so one might as well aim for the middle of the putting surface and have at it.

Too much club, however, and the ball can bound over the green into an unpleasant situation—be it tall grass, a bush or maybe up against a rock.

The green is a wide one, and a pin placement on the far left only increases the difficulty of an already difficult hole.

With the mountains rising up around the course and with pines coating the hillsides, the Rio Grande Club provides all things that are typically associated with mountain golf. And most of those things are very much in play at the 14th hole.

ROARING FORK

Club

16TH HOLE

177 yards • par 3

Basalt, Colorado 970•927•9000 www.roaringforkclub.com

Photograph by Dick Durrance II

The Roaring Fork Club provides two distinctly different atmospheres in which to play golf.

For the first five holes, the action takes place amidst panoramas typically found in the high ranchlands. The player then travels across to what is known as the "riverside" section of the course–where the trees often encroach, where the waters of the Roaring Fork River and Spring Creek come into play and where there are elevation changes not seen on the other portion of the course.

The last of the riverside holes is the 16th, a par 3 that forces a close encounter with the Roaring Fork River.

The river runs to the right of the back tee, creating as idyllic a scene as one could hope to find. And then the water encroaches all the way to the right edge of the green, thereby altering its demeanor from idyllic to menacing.

Trees on both sides of the hole create a funnel through which the tee shot must find its way, and that shot must also carry a wetlands-type area. The green is squeezed in between the river on the right and a bunker on the left.

It is all quite imposing, although one of the nearby hazards really doesn't come into play. One of the course's fishing ponds is short and left of the green–located in a spot where only the poorest of shots can find it.

The nine ponds at the Roaring Fork Club carry such names as Loch Ness and Bermuda Triangle. The one at the 16th hole is known as Kid's Pond.

It is designed for youngsters who are learning the fine art of angling, and it is the only body of water at the Roaring Fork Club where spin casting and bait may be used. The rest of the ponds and the river itself are devoted only to fly fishing.

Also at the Kid's Pond, each angler may keep one fish per day. The practice of "catch and release" is in force everywhere else on the property.

Unfortunately for those not fishing, the river does not catch and release the golf balls.

SHERATON STEAMBOAT

Golf Club

14TH HOLE

Photographs by Dave Thiemann

164 yards • par 3

Steamboat Springs, Colorado 970•879•1391 www.sheratonsteamboatgolf.com

The Sheraton Steamboat Golf Club was one of the forerunners in the sport's foray into the mountains, and it has an unmistakably mature look about it.

But, thanks to the surroundings, it looked like a mature course when it first opened in 1974.

Fish Creek flows through the property, and the views one comes to expect in this part of the world are available by the carload.

What strikes those who see this course for the first time, however, are the trees. That might seem odd since trees play such a key role on so many courses. But here the trees have an almost regal bearing, and they crowd in so close to the action that they must constantly be factored into a player's game plan.

Evergreens and aspens line most of the fairways, not only serving as a barrier between the golf and the world beyond, but also acting as a significant hazard. A ball that misses the fairway has a very good chance of being gathered up by the forest.

Even on the par-3 14th there are trees that pinch in on the field of play. But this is also one of the holes on which Fish Creek makes an appearance, thus creating a double header of problems on the tee shot.

The shot from the back tee must funnel its way between evergreens and then carry over the stream and its accompanying rocky border.

Two bunkers protect the right side of the green and the creek makes a turn so that it slides below and to the left of the putting surface. A shot that misses to the left can bound down the bank and plop into the water.

And surrounding the green are the ever-present trees, some of which climb up from the edge of the creek and stand ready to intercept a shot that has gone wayward.

At the 14th, as is the case all around this course, the woods create a look of elegance. But they also create the need to be precise.

SONNENALP

Resort of Vail

14TH HOLE

180 yards • par 3

Edwards, Colorado 970•477•5370 www.sonnenalp.com

Photograph by Ken Redding

There is always room for a little optical illusion on a golf course and the Sonnenalp Resort of Vail has a very nice example of visual trickery.

If a par 3 has a swale between the tee and the green, it is sometimes difficult to determine whether the shot is a little uphill or a little downhill. Club selection, after all, depends on the answer to this puzzle, and bad things can happen if the wrong club is selected.

The 14th at Sonnenalp, one of the nation's premier resort courses, carries with it this question.

There is a valley in front of the tee, and it is filled with brush and grasses. It is a deep enough valley to throw off the visual perception a little, even though it will take a very poor shot to put a ball into the hazard.

If one club too little is chosen, the ball can hit the grass slope in front of the green and fail to advance onto the putting surface. If one club too many is chosen, a trip into the back bunker might be in the offing and that is certainly no bargain.

So which is it?

The hole actually looks like it is perhaps a little bit uphill from the back tee. Except, of course, to those who think it is maybe just a wee bit downhill.

The answer turns out to be neither. Those who play Sonnenalp on a regular basis will testify to the fact that the green and tee are on almost exactly the same level. But they will also say that if the green is missed, it is best missed short rather than long. Unless it is missed short and left, which brings two bunkers built into the upslope into play.

And don't forget about the breezes, which are often in the face of the player on this hole. As all golfers know, there is no optical illusion when it comes to the wind.

BEAVER CREEK

Golf Club

15TH HOLE

Photographs by Dann Coffey

418 yards • par 4

Avon, Colorado 970•845•5775 www.beavercreek.snow.com

It does not take long to discover the key to playing the Beaver Creek Golf Club.

Hitting the ball straight is paramount. Some of the narrowest fairways in the state of Colorado are to be found below the ski slopes at Beaver Creek, a course set among the sumptuous dwellings that are synonymous with the community.

Robert Trent Jones Jr., one of the nation's most respected and sought-after architects, designed this mountain challenge, and he kept it short and not-so-sweet.

Even from the back tees, it plays at only 6,784 yards. By 21st-century standards, taking into account the advanced technology and the thinness of the local air, that yardage is easily handled by the long hitters.

But those long hitters had best hit it straight, especially at the par-4 15th.

The hole fits snugly amid towering trees on a mountainside that also contains condominiums and the ski slopes that become busy when the golf course is not.

The dramatic surroundings tend to dwarf the 15th fairway, which is already cozy enough. A drive from the slightly elevated tee need not be struck with a driver since preciseness is far more advantageous than distance. A creek runs down the right side of the fairway through the trees, but it takes a fairly wayward shot to find it.

There is a slight right-hand turn to the hole, after which a short iron will be needed to reach a green that is slightly higher than the fairway. Sizable bunkers protect the left front and the back right.

And well behind the green is a barn owned by the Holden family—natives of Scotland who ran a dairy farm on the property during the first few decades of the 20th century. The lady of the household died in the barn when she fell from a loft while gathering eggs.

Life at Beaver Creek is a lot less austere than it was when the Holdens were tending to their cows and chickens. But the golfers who stroll the fairways here quickly learn to follow a principle that guided the close-knit families who made a living in the mountains.

Those confronted by the tight fairways at Beaver Creek find they must to stick to the straight and narrow path.

BRECKENRIDGE

Golf Club

7TH HOLE

Elk Nine

Photographs by Bob Winsett

435 yards • par 4

Breckenridge, Colorado 970•453•9104 www.breckenridgegolfclub.com

Over the course of more than a decade of golfing seasons, the town of Breckenridge came to the collective conclusion that its 18-hole municipal course had become a very positive force for the community.

So Jack Nicklaus, who designed the layout, was asked back to create nine more holes. And when they opened in 2001, rave reviews followed.

It was dubbed the Elk Nine, and if it is combined with the Beaver Nine, they create a course with a slope rating of 151.

The United States Golf Association determines the slope rating for a course, and although a lot of factors go into it, suffice it to say that a slope of 151 is pretty high. The second highest in Colorado as it turns out.

There is much more elevation change on the Elk Nine than on Breckenridge's Beaver and Bear Nines, and the highest elevation of all is 9,445 feet. That is how far above sea level the seventh tee happens to be, and it is 85 feet from there down to the green.

But getting to the green on the par-4 seventh of the Elk Nine is no walk in the park.

The prominent attraction as seen from the tee box is what appears to be a wall of pines off in the distance. Much farther away still are the mountains, casting their enchantment over the high valley.

A big drive aimed at the distant trees is called for. With a hint of fade added in, the ball will bound down and down the fairway as it makes a right-hand sweep to a point, hopefully, short of a ravine that is the chief feature of the hole.

Only the longest hitters need to gear down a little to make sure the tee shot does not reach the chasm.

The second shot is over the rough-filled ditch to a saucer-like green sitting beyond the trees that were so menacing from the tee. To the right of the green is a slope that falls back into the hazard, and two bunkers reside on the hillside in order to catch errant shots before they can get away completely.

Just seeing this hole is enough to be convinced that the residents of Breckenridge were quite correct in calling on Nicklaus to conjure up nine more for them.

THE BRIDGES

Golf & Country Club

13TH HOLE

349 yards • par 4

Montrose, Colorado 970•252•1119 www.montrosebridges.com

Photograph by Dick Durrance II

There are 10 lakes and 85 bunkers, many of the traps being of the giant, economy size.

Earth (850,000 cubic yards of it) has been moved, and sod (two million-square-feet worth) has been planted.

No, it is not Palm Springs. Yes, it is Montrose, just down the road from the Black Canyon of the Gunnison, where Jack Nicklaus has created what those who live there like to describe as a "lavish course design."

That it is. With its five sets of tees, the layout gives the amateur a chance and the professional a test.

The Bridges Golf & Country Club is named for the 17 bridges of all sizes and descriptions that are needed to cross over the water hazards that come into play on 16 holes.

During the course of play there will come into view waterfalls, boulders, waste areas with native vegetation, arroyos and, as a constant reminder of just where you are, that being the nearby mountains.

There is also a variety of holes, including a short par 4 on which water and sand are very prominent.

The 13th at The Bridges, as any hole that does not require length should, calls for a certain amount of precision.

Bunkers are in evidence down the right side of the fairway, and water is on the left. Neither hazard is an appetizing prospect, although the sand clearly does less short-term damage to the scorecard.

The approach shot must carry over a pond and between the water and the green is a bunker of expansive proportion. There is sand behind the green as well, and the putting surface is large and rambling.

A second shot that does not come to rest within a reasonable distance from the cup will usually lead to a first putt that requires much thought and a deft touch.

Finally, directly behind the hole and seemingly within touching distance, are the Rockies in all their grandeur.

Nicklaus always leaves behind a course worth seeing as well as worth playing, and the 13th at The Bridges tells us he has done just that on the Western Slope.

THE BRIDGES

Golf & Country Club

18TH HOLE

444 yards • par 4

Montrose, Colorado 970•252•1119 www.montrosebridges.com

Photograph by Dick Durrance II

There are, to be sure, eye-catching novelties to be found at The Bridges Golf & Country Club.

The back tee on the very first hole, for instance, is part of the same piece of precisely mown grass that makes up the putting green.

Holes No. 2 and No. 11 share the same tee box. And at the par-5 15th there are two greens. Some days the hole is 572 yards long. On other occasions it plays 600 yards with the approach shot having to carry over a canal.

But in between all the clever design features, there is lots and lots of pure golf. And it does not get much purer than the challenge architect Jack Nicklaus has saved for last.

As he usually does when a tee shot requires a full-bore effort, Nicklaus has left quite a bit of room for the drive at the par-4 18th to find a safe spot.

But anything wide left will get wet. Water, as it does on all but two holes at The Bridges, comes very much into play. In this case, it travels down the entire left side and eventually spreads across the face of the green.

Even the big hitters need a solid smack from the back tee to set up a second shot in the 150- to 170-yard range.

In addition to the water, sand hovers around the edges of the green, which has a hump running through it that creates two distinct sections. The green also generally slopes back to the water, but because of the length and severity of the hole, hitting any part of the putting surface in regulation is reason for applause.

Immediately behind the 18th green is the facility's distinctive clubhouse—a rambling two-story structure that gives off the feeling of a ranch house built along space-aged lines.

The clubhouse fits right into a course that contains a multitude of very individualistic features, but which also calls for golf of a skillful nature, especially on the last hole of the day.

CATAMOUNT

Ranch & Club

12TH HOLE

341 yards • par 4

Steamboat Springs, Colorado 970•871•9200 www.catamountranchclub.com

Photograph by David Thiemann

One of the more recognizable identifying marks in all the world of golf design involves Tom Weiskopf and his short par 4s.

He has one on each of his courses and they are never dull, although given the surroundings into which the Catamount Ranch & Club has been placed it would have been virtually impossible to build a dull hole.

The most significant feature of any short par 4 is that it is, in a word, short. But any abbreviated par 4 worth its salt also features very small areas in which the ball can come to rest and still be out of harm's way.

If a decision is made at the tee to try to reach the green in a single shot, which is always the lure, those small areas can become even smaller, which is always the risk.

Weiskopf has constructed a bunch of short par 4s at Catamount Ranch. The fifth plays less than 300 yards with the green all but surrounded by sand. The sixth is also short of 300 yards and features a wetlands area about 80 yards from the green.

And then there is the 12th, which is 341 yards from the back. But because the tee is elevated, it is possible to put a tee shot very close to, if not on, the green.

That tee shot must also carry over a field of native vegetation that continues to take up space along the entire left side of the fairway—looking very much like the kind of growth found on courses in Hawaii.

Out in the fairway itself are bunkers surrounding the kind of narrow, confined landing area typically found on a short par 4.

The green, which has sand all across the front, is wide and not very deep, creating the need for preciseness on the short second shot.

A vegetation-covered hillside dominates the scene to the right of the fairway, and beyond the hole the ground surges upward with layer after layer of pines stretching to the sky. It is a wonderful example of how a golf hole can accentuate, rather than diminish, the surrounding magnificence.

In other words, the 12th hole at Catamount Ranch is short on distance, but very, very long on allure.

COPPER CREEK

Golf

4TH HOLE

441 yards • par 4

Copper Mountain, Colorado 970•968•3333 www.coppercolorado.com

Photograph courtesy of Copper Creek Golf

There are plenty of places to play golf in Colorado where the elevation is significant. But it is more significant at Copper Creek Golf than anywhere else in the state. Or the country for that matter.

At 9,700 feet above sea level, Copper Creek is North America's highest 18-hole golf course. Designed by Pete and Perry Dye and dedicated to the premise that a perfect round is equal parts casual and challenging, friendly and formidable, Copper Creek is certain to delight.

There are giant pines. There is water to avoid in the form of both lakes and streams. Railroad ties, the well-known Dye trademark, are sprinkled about. There are even the remains of a mining town that prospered during the 19th century.

The flattest holes on the course—the fourth through the seventh—are the ones that are farthest from the base of Copper Mountain. And they also provide the best vantage point to take in the wonderful views of Ten Mile Range.

This stretch of holes begins with the longest par 4 on the course, one that requires accuracy in addition to length.

A wetland runs down the left side, and rough that is maintained at a troublesome length is on the right. There is simply no good place to be except on the short grass.

The second shot needs to avoid a lone bunker on the front right corner of the green and there is water behind the putting surface to catch the ball that has sailed through the extra-thin air a little more than was anticipated.

The green itself is not dramatically undulating, but there are enough subtle slopes to put pressure on the player's ability to properly judge a putt.

Copper Creek's back nine is carved out of the pine forest and involves a trip up the mountainside and down again with the relics of the area's mining past appearing along the way.

While nature provides the setting, it's the people who provide the service and enhance the experience. The colorful cast of characters create a "welcome, enjoy, and come back soon" atmosphere.

A trip up and down this mountainside, of course, is another of the chief lures at Copper Creek. After all, when seeking out a personable, unpretentious, high-quality alpine golfing experience, it is nice to be able to say you found one that is higher than any other one.

THE CLUB AT CORDILLERA

14TH HOLE
The Summit Course

412 yards • par 4

Edwards, Colorado 970•926•5300 www.cordillera-vail.com

Photograph by Henebry Photography

In the midst of Colorado's mountain resort world, The Club at Cordillera provides it all when it comes to getting away.

Jack Nicklaus was not originally sure, however, if Cordillera needed any more golf than it already had.

Before Nicklaus was hired to work his magic, three courses had been constructed in connection with the resort. There was the Mountain Course (designed by Hale Irwin), the Valley Course (a work of Tom Fazio) and the Short Course (put together by putting guru Dave Pelz).

Nicklaus was asked to build another course at the very top of the mountain, 9,200 feet high, a layout to be known as The Summit Course.

"The first time I saw the property and how exposed it would be to wind and weather, I asked Cordillera if they were sure they wanted to put a golf course up here," Nicklaus said, the day he unveiled his handiwork by playing an introductory round. "Then the longer we looked and the longer we thought, the more we knew that it would work."

The product turned out to be every bit as spectacular as one would have expected it to be.

"This is the only golf course on which you can seemingly see forever from each hole," the architect said.

The par-4 14th is a prime example. The hole begins with a tee shot to a generous bowl-shaped fairway, giving the player a sense of confidence while standing on the tee.

A bunker centered at the end of the landing area provides an excellent target for alignment, with natural grasses and aspens clogging the nearby hillsides.

A solid drive leaves the player an uphill approach to a two-level green guarded on the front left by a single bunker.

As players exit the green, they will experience one of the views that Nicklaus refers to. The vistas to the south looking back down the fairway indeed make one feel they can just about see forever. And even if they can't, they will be very glad that Nicklaus finally decided the property was, after all, fit for one more golf course.

COUNTRY CLUB OF THE ROCKIES

12TH HOLE

477 yards • par 4

Edwards, Colorado 970•926•3080 www.countrycluboftherockies.com

Photograph by Tony Chesla

The Eagle River can be seen running alongside, and occasionally underneath, Interstate Highway 70.

And it is revealed in its full glory on the golf course at the Country Club of the Rockies, where it makes an appearance on four holes and adds a special dimension to the Jack Nicklaus design that drifts through the rolling mountain terrain.

If only superior shots are hit at the par-4 12th, the Eagle River will likely not come into play. The water, nevertheless, must be crossed and stands ready to collect the shots that are not struck with the center of the club face.

This is the longest par 4 on the course, and there are not many longer in all of the Rockies.

From the tee the player can admire an expansive view of Vail Mountain, and after doing that there must be a tee shot that is hit with authority.

The always-lurking native grasses are to the left of the fairway, and out of bounds is to the right. It is a slightly downhill drive and the prevailing wind helps, which is certainly a plus on a hole this long.

It is on the second shot that the Eagle River asserts itself. It babbles across the fairway about 100 yards short of the green, and if the tee shot has been mis-hit, it becomes a formidable challenge to carry the water.

Pine trees are found between the river and the green, acting like goal posts between which the ball must be guided.

Oversized rocks are also sprinkled around to within about 50 yards from the green. A shot that barely gets over the river might confront one of the stones and bound off to who knows where.

There are no bunkers in front of the green, which on a Nicklaus course is not all that usual. But because this is such a long hole, the architect has given the player a break around the putting surface.

It is enough, apparently, to have survived the rigors of almost 500 yards of risk as well as a crossing of the Eagle River.

DEVIL'S THUMB

13TH HOLE

411 yards • par 4

Delta, Colorado 970•874•6262 www.deltagolf.org

Photograph by Tony Bohling

It would be easy to refer to any number of courses in Colorado as "unique." But when it comes to Devil's Thumb, no other word would do.

"When I first looked at the property, I didn't think there was any way to build a golf course there," said Rick Phelps, the man who designed what turned out to be a very special layout.

Phelps calls it a "prairie-style" course, and it was made possible only because an abandoned pipeline was repaired and used to bring snowmelt down from the nearby higher elevations so the fairways and greens could be watered.

Now the community-owned course is a major attraction for those who enjoy a golfing experience that does not come along just every day.

There is no better example of what Devil's Thumb is all about than the par-4 13th.

From a tee elevated about 100 feet above the green, the vastness of the surroundings is visible. The desert-like landscape is all around, and off in the distance are the formations that carry exotic names such as the Uncompahgre Plateau.

Down below, meanwhile, is the green, which can be reached two ways.

There is a fairway, built on the same level as the tee, to the right of the ultimate target. Once on the fairway, the player turns left and aims at a green built into a sort of saddle between two forbidding hillsides.

Most who play this hole, however, ignore the fairway and go right at the green. If the direct route is chosen, the yardage to the hole is considerably less than that listed on the scorecard. But it is a route fraught with peril.

An area of maintained grass has been created short of the green, but anything short of that will wind up in the desert. It is possible to draw a playable lie on the hardpan, but it is also possible for the ball to find a very unpleasant spot in which to settle.

The green itself rises to a crest in the middle and then falls away on the other side of the high point. That brings about the chance for a roller coaster putt. There are three bunkers short and left of the green and another one short and right.

It is, to say the least, not an ordinary hole. Which is the way it should be since Devil's Thumb is a long way from being an ordinary golf course.

LAKOTA CANYON RANCH

Golf Club

16TH HOLE

418 yards • par 4

New Castle, Colorado 970•984•9700 www.lakotacanyonranch.com

Photographs by Dick Durrance II

The unmistakable hand of architect Jim Engh has been brought to bear on the land in the shadow of Burning Mountain.

At the Lakota Canyon Ranch Golf Club, residents of a fast-growing section of the state have been provided a golfing experience worthy of any spot in the country.

The canyon-filled countryside in Garfield County, of course, does not resemble just any spot in the country. Golf holes laid out on this kind of terrain almost automatically become spectacular, especially when the architect is one used to dealing with such impressive settings.

The entire course is striking, but the three-hole closing stretch is particularly so.

It begins with a par 4 where the area's natural beauty becomes a significant part of the playing process.

From the elevated tee, the chief feature of the hole is easily seen. It is a ravine, filled with all the undergrowth and rough ground one would expect to see in a ravine.

The depression runs down the right side of the fairway, so the tendency is to favor the left portion of the landing area. But the farther left of center the ball travels, the longer the second shot becomes. And the second shot is the one that makes or breaks the score on this hole.

The hole doglegs sharply to the right, meaning the approach shot has to clear the ravine. It must also stay clear of a very penal and very large bunker that sits below and in front of the green. The trap first appears about 35 yards shy of the putting surface and runs about a third of the way along its left side.

High grass walls rim the bunker, an Engh trademark.

The green itself has been carved out of a hillside, creating an arena-like look with the rugged landscape overseeing the action from above.

In the background is Burning Mountain, the immense rock outcropping that towers over the town of New Castle and provides another example of why Lakota Canyon Ranch sits on something other than ordinary ground.

MAROON CREEK

Club

12TH HOLE

490 yards • par 4

Aspen, Colorado 970•920•1533

Photograph by Dick Durrance II

When it comes to discussions about which hole might be at the top of a particular golfing list, there can never be any real winners.

There is only debate. Or, sometimes, honest-to-goodness arguments. That's the way golf is.

As far as the most difficult hole in Colorado is concerned, for instance, there might be an assortment of contenders. And one of them can certainly be found at the Maroon Creek Club near Aspen, where even those with the highest-quality golfing attributes are tested by the par-4 12th.

It is a dazzling hole, on top of being very, very challenging. Its splendor sprawls out over a hillside with both man-made and natural hazards in abundance. There is even a classic babbling brook thrown into the mix.

At 490 yards from the back tee, the hole obviously has length. But it has a lot more than that.

The idea with the drive is to hit the ball as far as you can. Straight is also recommended.

Willow Creek runs to the left of the fairway with very tall natural grasses alongside, and there is rough to the right.

The creek then makes a turn and crosses the fairway, and if the tee ball is struck along the ideal line it takes a drive of about 340 yards to get to the water. Then the fun starts.

The second shot is steeply uphill and all carry. There is grass cut to fairway length all the way up the hill to the green, but it is to the left of the direct line to the putting surface.

In order to reach the green on the fly, the ball must carry over a nest of eight bunkers cut into the slope. It makes for a formidable sight, indeed, along with requiring a formidable shot.

There is more work to be done because the green has two distinct levels separated by a ridge. A large mound acts as a backstop to the left of the green and the hill into which the green is built continues to go up and up into the tall grasses and trees.

It is a hole built on a scale northing short of magnificent, and it also becomes apparent during its playing that it is worthy of being considered among the hardest in all of the state.

POLE CREEK

Golf Club

4TH HOLE

The Ridge Nine

443 yards • par 4

Winter Park, Colorado 970•887•9195 www.polecreekgolf.com

Photograph by Byron Hetzler

There is a varied golfing experience to be found at the Pole Creek Club, where three award-winning nine-hole courses are tucked in among the other outdoor activities that abound in the shadow of Rocky Mountain National Park.

The Meadow Nine and Ranch Nine have been constructed in, appropriately enough, meadows and ranchland with the pines pinching in from time to time to add to the challenge.

There is also the Ridge Nine, which delivers elevation changes and what head professional J.T. Thompson calls, "the most spectacular view in Colorado."

In a locale where merely opening one's back door can provide stunning scenery, that is quite a statement. But after a trip around the Ridge Nine, it would be hard to argue with the pro's assessment.

From the elevated tee at the ninth, for instance, various peaks are visible at various distances with an ocean of pines stretching out to reach the mountains.

The view at the fourth isn't bad, either.

At the fourth, there appears to be all the room in the world into which to hit a tee shot. There are pines everywhere, of course, but they are not confining. The urge becomes overwhelming to grab the driver and whale away.

The tee shot is also downhill, cascading along to a relatively wide landing area.

Watching a well-struck shot from any tee box in the world provides the kind of goosebumps that are singular with golf, but a drive that soars into the limitless blue sky of a mountain course is extra special.

As is almost always the case in golf, however, things soon toughen up a little.

The tee shot actually needs to be directed to the right center of the fairway in order to have the best angle to the green, which is located behind a large pond. The water does not run all the way to the green, and there is room out to the right if there is a desire to play the second shot ultra safe.

Nevertheless, the pond is a major player if the approach is to be placed anywhere near the hole.

There are no bunkers to get in the way around the wide green, but none are needed. They would only mar a scene of golfing beauty that some feel cannot be topped anywhere.

RED SKY

Ranch & Golf Club

14TH HOLE

Fazio Course

400 yards • par 4

Wolcott, Colorado 866•873•3759 www.redskygolfclub.com

Photograph by Allen Kennedy

Having two glorious golf courses as part of the same property is certainly a luxury, and having them designed by different masters of the trade is even more so.

Of course, it doesn't hurt that the property in question is the sort of ground on which Red Sky Ranch is located and where Greg Norman and Tom Fazio have worked their architectural magic.

"Red Sky not only provides the opportunity to play great golf, but also to encounter dramatic Rocky Mountain landscapes in their pure environmental forms," Fazio said when his work opened for play.

His team was so concerned about making sure the natural vegetation was protected, more than 23,000 plants were moved from the course, cared for in nurseries and then brought back and planted around as the 18 holes began to emerge.

But what Fazio did best of all was take full advantage of the shape of the land, something he does with unsurpassed excellence.

There is no better illustration of using the land to your advantage than Fazio's 14th hole at Red Sky Ranch. It's almost like spreading paint on a wall. The architect "simply" coated the rolling ground with a different mixture of grass, sand and vegetation and turned golfers loose on it.

The tee shot on the medium-length par-4 travels over a slight rise, past a grove of aspen on the left and out onto a broad plain of fairway which, in turn, makes a sweeping arc to the left. It all fits into the theme of vastness which symbolizes the place.

Up ahead is the green, which sits on the edge of a ridge. A mound to the right of the green actually drifts onto the putting surface, creating a back-right pin placement that takes an ultra-precise shot to get near.

It is to the left of the green, however, where the major action is found. The ground falls away on the left side, and as it does so it is occupied by three bunkers that can actually serve as prevention for major problems. If a shot soars to the left of the green and misses the bunkers, it can tumble down the slope into a whole catalogue of woe.

The gentle sweep of this terrain has been unchanged since the Rockies were formed and it remains unchanged today. The only difference now is that there is a golf hole sitting on it.

RIO GRANDE

Club & Golf Course

1 ST HOLE

450 yards • par 4

South Fork, Colorado 719•873•1995 www.riograndeclub.com

Photograph by Ken May, Rolling Greens Photography

Since first impressions are always important, attempts are usually made in the world of golf architecture to give the player something pleasant to look at from the first tee.

Maybe even memorable.

For the most part that is not very hard to do in Colorado, but it is really hard to beat the first impression one gets at the Rio Grande Club.

Created at the base of Wolf Creek Pass, the Rio Grande Club winds its way through rugged ground that encourages the player to keep the ball on the fairway.

And there is no more rugged ground to be found on the course than that which is visible on the very first hole.

Stretching out below the elevated opening tee is a ribbon of fairway heading off to a green that is very much within view a quarter of a mile away. There is a fairly typical sort of rough to the left of the fairway—a mixture of native grasses and uneven ground that will almost certainly bring about an undesirable lie for the second shot.

But the problems to the left do not begin to compare with the difficulties that await on the right.

All down the right side of the fairway is nothing less than a rocky wall. It is the face of a dramatic hillside that goes almost straight up. Growing out of the rock here and there are small trees and bushes, and the entire scene is simply forbidding.

A shot that heads to the right even the slightest bit will slam into the rock, and then it is anybody's guess.

There is always the possibility that the natural barrier, because it is so steep, will simply act as a backboard and cause the ball to bounce back to the fairway and wind up in reasonably decent shape. Any time that happens, however, the ball will pick up a scratch or two.

But there is the chance that, after bouncing around the rocks for a bit, the ball might lodge somewhere in a tree or in a crevice. Or it might bounce crazily back toward the tee.

The best idea is to avoid all that by finding the fairway, after which the second shot is directed toward a green protected in front and to the left by bunkers. And just to the right of the green is that wall of rock, still very much in play.

From the tee to the green, the very unique wall at the Rio Grande Club makes a stirring first impression.

ROARING FORK
Club

6TH HOLE

360 yards • par 4

Basalt, Colorado 970•927•9000 www.roaringforkclub.com

Photograph by Dick Durrance II

To the surprise of golf's most impassioned practitioners, the great outdoors can sometimes be put to other uses.

Those who partake of the various splendors at the Roaring Fork Club can attest to that.

There is the golf, naturally, which is available in the kind of setting that automatically lures people to the game.

And then there is the fishing, which is given equal billing at Roaring Fork Club for reasons that soon become apparent.

The Roaring Fork River, which knifes through the center of the course, provides fly fishing opportunities on a grand scale. There are also the nine ponds scattered around the property, each of them laden with trout. So if that chronic slice has made an unwelcome return, there is an available option not enjoyed at most courses.

That option is very much in play at the par-4 sixth, where the Roaring Fork River is first encountered.

The river runs down the right side of the fairway for the entire length of the hole, but the back tee is placed to the right of the water. That forces a carry over the rock-lined river at an angle–always an awkward endeavor. The tee shot must also soar between two tall cottonwoods that serve as a gateway to the landing area.

Long hitters will likely use something less than a driver, even from the back tee, because accuracy is far more vital than distance.

If the river and the trees have been avoided off the tee, a relatively short second shot is left. But it must carry over yet another body of water. Spring Creek ambles in front of the green and spills into the nearby river, creating a final opportunity on this hole for nature to get in the way of the golf.

The recently rebuilt putting surface is narrow, not all that deep and features a hump in the back section that adds to the task at hand–especially when the pin is placed nearby. A bunker guards the left side and wraps around behind, and it all nestles in among the towering trees.

It is an ideal location for not one, but two forms of recreation that, at Roaring Fork, are equally encouraged.

SONNENALP

Resort of Vail

10TH HOLE

414 yards • par 4

Edwards, Colorado 970•477•5370 www.sonnenalp.com

Photograph by Ken Redding

The one obvious drawback with mountain golf is that there cannot be any mountain golf during certain months of the year.

At Vail's Sonnenalp Resort, however, its down-valley location usually allows the sport to be played all the way into late October. And that is a good thing because of Sonnenalp's reputation as one of the top resort courses in the United States.

The layout drifts through sharply rising hills and past the kind of lovely homes that act as a lure to those anxious to flee the metropolitan bustle.

And if tranquility is, indeed, being sought, the 10th hole at Sonnenalp is a pretty good place to land.

It is a hole that capitalizes on the wide open spaces. There is a massive fairway, and there is but a single bunker on the entire hole.

The difficulty, however, lies in the fact the hole plays slightly uphill and that the green is narrow and slopes sharply from back to front.

So even though there is a great deal of room in which to put the tee shot, that shot must be struck with authority.

This is not a hole on which length can be ignored for accuracy's sake. The big hitters have a distinct advantage, and those who are not big hitters must guard against trying to smash the ball farther than they are capable. Making an overly aggressive swing invariably leads to trouble.

The wide fairway pitches and rolls so that a level lie for the second shot is a rarity. And because of a big hill on the right, the fairway slopes to the left.

It is possible to bounce the ball onto the green, but it is imperative to avoid the deep bunker on the left side of the putting surface. Although it is the only trap on the hole, it is a major hazard.

The 10th at Sonnenalp can be a forgiving hole because of the width of the fairway, but it takes two big shots to reach the green in regulation. And the good news is that it can be played a little deeper into the season than many holes in this part of the world.

ASPEN GLEN

Golf Club

6TH HOLE

560 yards • par 5

Carbondale, Colorado 970•704•1988 www.aspen-glen.com

Photograph by Dick Durrance II

A second generation of the Nicklaus family is hard at work in the golf design business, and the proof can be found beneath the snow-capped peak of Mount Sopris.

It is the Aspen Glen Golf Club, where Jack Nicklaus and Jack Nicklaus II teamed up to build a course in a neighborhood where trout spawn and eagles nest.

"It is one of the finest golf courses in which the Nicklaus family has been privileged to be involved," the elder of the two designers said.

The Roaring Fork River comes into play on eight holes and encircles the entire putting surface at the 18th, making it the state's only natural island green.

For pure beauty, however, it is hard to beat the par-5 sixth—a broad swath of emerald turf dotted with mounded bunkers and a rock-strewn stream that slices the fairway in two. It is the kind of hole that inspires the player to strike good shots simply out of respect for its splendor.

There is a reasonably ample amount of room off the tee with the task here being to put the ball in position so that the hole's key hazard can be dealt with on the second shot.

There are two bunkers to the right of the fairway that must be avoided off the tee, and if the wind is helping, the longest hitters need to make sure they don't drive the ball too far.

A massive blast might, with its final bounce, jump into the creek that runs across the fairway.

Getting as close to the water as possible off the tee, of course, is the best way to take pressure off the second shot, with which the creek needs to be carried en route to a position of safety between the bunkers that dominate the scene close to the green.

The bunkers line both sides of the fairway, and the closer the player gets to the green with the second shot, the less room there is between the clusters of sand.

The ball can be bounced onto the green between the last of the bunkers, but there is a lot of putting surface and the cup is often tucked behind a trap on either the extreme right or left side.

With Mount Sopris providing the backdrop, a golfing treat has been created by not one, but two members of clan Nicklaus.

BRECKENRIDGE

Golf Club

8TH HOLE

Beaver Nine

Photographs by Bob Winsett

580 yards • par 5

Breckenridge, Colorado 970•453•9104 www.breckenridgegolfclub.com

Not enough credit in the world of golf is given to wildlife.

The Old Course at St. Andrews, for instance, owes a large debt to the sheep who burrowed into the dunes to make the bunkers and who kept the grass conveniently trimmed before the days of lawn mowers.

Due homage should be given as well to the beavers at Breckenridge. There are elk roaming around and red fox are all over the place, along with the occasional moose. A bear is even spotted from time to time.

But the beavers are the ones who created the ponds on one of the three nine-hole courses laid out by the Jack Nicklaus design firm. Those courses are known as the Elk, Bear and, in proper tribute, the Beaver.

There is a lovely example of the amphibious rodents' work on the par-5 eighth of the Beaver Nine, which drifts along at an elevation of 9,324 feet between pine-laden hillsides and rows of small trees and tall shrubs.

The chief chore on each of the first two shots is to stay away from all the vegetation, find the verdant, flat fairway and leave a relatively short distance for the approach to the green.

It is on that third shot that the beaver pond is encountered. The pond is not all that large, but it is surrounded by multi-colored grasses, low growing shrubs and a few mid-sized trees.

The pond also attracts golf balls by the bushel.

The green angles away from the player with less distance required to reach the right-hand portion than it does to get to the left side. The pond follows the angle of the green so that no matter where the pin is located, the approach shot is all carry over the water.

There are design features on many Nicklaus courses which might look natural but which are the work of big pieces of machinery and many, many man hours.

But at Breckenridge, a lot of the labor was put in by generations' worth of furry creatures.

COUNTRY CLUB OF THE ROCKIES

13TH HOLE

573 yards • par 5

Edwards, Colorado 970•926•3080 www.countrycluboftherockies.com

Photograph by Tony Chesla

The mountains that are such an overpowering factor in much of Colorado golf are hard to ignore, especially at such locations as the Country Club of the Rockies.

But now and then a hole is encountered that would be considered a work of grandeur even if it happened to be located off in the flatlands. The par-5 13th at this Jack Nicklaus-designed layout is just such a spot.

One of the most pleasing scenes in all of golf is a fairway that extends for hundreds of yards into the distance without any major obstacles directly in the way. That is the case at the 13th, where the beautifully maintained grass acts as a lure—encouraging the player to make a lurch-free swing so that the ball will eventually appear off in the distance bounding along the carpet.

That's not to say there isn't trouble. The Eagle River, with trees growing alongside its banks, travels the entire length of the hole on the right side.

Walls of rock shoot up over on the left, creating a course boundary. They are very much in play for a shot hit sharply in that direction.

The fairway is contoured only in a subtle manner. There are no big elevation changes and it does not tilt heavily to the right or left. Instead of being pummeled, the player is treated to a gentle massage.

The action picks up around the green, where there are bunkers to the left, right and beyond. And when the wind blows, which it does more often than not, it is usually in the player's face.

On a calm day, however, those who hit the ball a long way might have a go at the green in two. It is, after all, a user-friendly hole—one that would be welcome on any course, regardless of its altitude or lack of it.

DALTON RANCH

Golf Club

16TH HOLE

514 yards • par 5

Durango, Colorado 970•247•8774 www.daltonranch.com

Photographs by Chris Giles

The journey along the famed Durango and Silverton Narrow Gauge Railroad is about 50 miles, and the ratio of grandeur per mile makes it one of the more fascinating tourist attractions in the country.

For golfers, however, there is one particular part of the trip that stands out.

Six miles north of Durango, the train and its passengers roll past the sixth, seventh, 13th and 14th holes of the Dalton Ranch Golf Club.

That allows for a preview of what is in store for those who venture out onto the Ken Dye-designed course, placed alongside the Animas River and below the red cliffs of the San Juan Mountains.

For the most part at Dalton Ranch, there is ample room off the tees, but the approach shots are routinely demanding because of the elevation found on many of the greens, as well as the deep bunkering around them.

When it comes to tee shots, however, the par-5 16th provides an exception. The landing area is reduced in size by an unusual design feature that is planted right in the middle of the fairway.

It is a grass bunker, about 30 yards long and deeper than a player is tall. But if reaching the green in two is the goal, the grass bunker must be cleared. The tee shot must also get past a sand bunker on the left edge of the fairway—one that is longer than the grass bunker and just as deep.

If the tee shot can make it over those two obstacles, it can catch a downslope and roll out to within 175 to 200 yards of the green. And from there the second shot becomes fairly routine.

Those playing the hole in the traditional manner can stay short of or to the right of the grass bunker and then lay up, being careful to avoid a trap on the right side of the fairway that is about 100 yards from the green.

The green is protected in front by a group of traps, including a pot bunker at the very front center. The Animas River runs to the right of the green, but it takes a fairly loose shot to reach it.

The town of Durango is well known as being the jumping-off place for one of the great train rides in the land—one that is an official historic landmark. Now it is becoming known as well for offering those, who are so inclined, a gorgeous golfing ride.

THE RIVER COURSE

at Keystone

18TH HOLE

520 yards • par 5

Keystone, Colorado 800•464•3494 www.golfkeystone.com

Photograph by Jack Affleck

While playing the front nine at Keystone's Hordzan/Fry-designed River Course, there are multiple encounters with the charms of the Snake River.

But the back nine leaves the riverside and marches its way through a forest of lodgepole pines. Along the way are some of the most impressive elevation changes in all of Colorado golf, which is saying something.

There is a dizzying 194-foot drop, for instance, between the tee and green at the par-4 16th hole. And while it is not that far down to the fairway from the 18th tee, there is a decided slope involved.

After playing 17 holes on The River Course, the player is rewarded with a gorgeous view of Lake Dillon from the teeing ground on the 18th, and the view down to the fairway isn't bad, either.

On both sides of the fairway are the pines, forming very distinct borders within which the tee shot must be kept. The drive also has to carry an area of grassland to reach the fairway, but if the appropriate tee has been used that should be no problem because of the sharply downhill nature of the ground.

The latter portion of the hole swings back uphill, and although it is not as much uphill as the tee shot was downhill, the shape of the land is still a factor when it comes to club selection.

The bunkers are a factor as well.

From about 110 yards to the green there are a dozen traps. They pinch in on both sides of the typical landing area for a second shot layup, and they come into play as well for the player who attempts to reach the green in two and hits a shot that does not quite come off.

A third shot of close to 100 yards from one of those bunkers sharply decreases the odds for a par.

The last three bunkers guard the front, the right side and the back of the green, which sits in front of yet another row of pines.

Although the final hole at The River Course ends with a brief uphill climb, it is the downhill vistas on the back nine that will leave a very large impression.

LAKOTA CANYON RANCH

Golf Club

18TH HOLE

557 yards • par 5

New Castle, Colorado 970•984•9700 www.lakotacanyonranch.com

Photograph by Dick Durrance II

The seemingly inhospitable but starkly beautiful ground around New Castle was once occupied chiefly by coal miners, whose existence was anything but bountiful.

Imagine what those who toiled in such grim circumstances might think of those who enjoy a crystal clear day in hopes of mining a birdie or two.

Actually, from a golfing standpoint, the closing hole at Lakota Canyon Ranch Golf Club is fairly hard work, too.

The laborers' hands might not get all that dirty, but there could be some smudges left on the psyche if the ball strays into the wasteland.

Lakota's 18th is a par 5 and opens with a forced carry over one of the ravines that wind through the property. The ravine then makes a turn and continues down the right side of the fairway.

A big drive allows the bombers to go for the narrow green in two, although such a shot is all carry over about 100 yards of grassland that fronts the putting surface.

Those who do not hit the ball massive distances face a decision for their second shot. It is possible to aim for a second fairway built over to the right of the main one. Such a shot, if struck with absolute precision, can reduce the distance left for the approach to the green.

But to get to that alternate fairway, the shot must carry over the ravine to a smallish target protected by a bunker. The ravine must then be cleared again with the third shot, and from that angle the green is very, very shallow.

Most players will lay up with their second shot short of the grassy area about 150 yards from the green and then go for it from there–being careful to avoid the ravine, which creeps up to the right edge of the target, and the slope of a hill that rises up to the left.

It is a complicated sort of hole that comes at the end of the day when both mental and physical weariness might have set in.

Playing the 18th, however, is probably a little easier than mining coal.

POLE CREEK

Golf Club

2ND HOLE

The Meadow Nine

534 yards • par 5

Winter Park, Colorado 970•887•9195 www.polecreekgolf.com

Photograph by Byron Hetzler

When the Pole Creek Golf Club opened in 1985, a national magazine devoted to the sport named the course the best new public golfing facility in the nation.

That was strong praise, and accolades have continued to pour in for a destination that ranks as high as is possible on the entertainment meter.

Three nine-hole layouts present a combination of challenge and charm. And since Rocky Mountain National Park is the primary backdrop, the views speak for themselves.

If The Meadow Nine is chosen to start the day's play, the opening hole offers a chance to ease into the action with a comfortably wide fairway in which to place the first shot.

But things change in a hurry.

The towering lodgepole pines that are such a chief component at Pole Creek become a factor at the par-5 second.

The view from the second tee is both menacing and magnificent. The elegant pines rise up far into the distance and they encroach very near the fairway. If a tee shot is usually played with a draw or fade, it had best be only a slight draw or fade. Instead, something along the lines of absolutely straight would be recommended or the crack of ball hitting wood will soon be echoing across the land.

In addition to the imposing trees, a gap on the left side of the fairway has been created for a bunker that runs for almost 30 yards and can inhale a tee shot that has been struck with authority but which has drifted slightly off line.

The pines remain a factor all the way to the green, but if two solid shots have been struck there will be only a short third to a target that is protected by a large bunker across the front.

One of the side effects of playing mountain golf is that solitude is readily available. With the trees closing in to such a degree, it would be hard to find a golfing locale with more solitude than the second hole at Pole Creek's Meadow Nine.

THE GOLF CLUB AT REDLANDS MESA

5TH HOLE

575 yards • par 5

Grand Junction, Colorado 866•863•9270 www.redlandsmesa.com

Photograph by Dick Durrance II

Sitting as it does alongside the Colorado National Monument, the Golf Club at Redlands Mesa carries with it some of the most striking scenery in all of the United States.

One national magazine likened it to playing golf at the bottom of the Grand Canyon.

Walls of pink and red sandstone tower over the scene, piles of boulders litter the landscape and the occasional eagle soars by. And then there is the golf, blended into the environment by architect Jim Engh.

The par-5 fifth hole is no less than a golfing tour de force, featuring a variety of shot selections as well as a variety of landmarks.

From the Monument Tee, the hole plays to a fairly robust 575 yards, and the drive must carry over a huge rock outcropping and then down into the safety of the fairway. Off in the distance is a bunker that signals the point at which the fairway makes a right turn, and that bunker is a good aiming point off the tee.

If the fairway is missed, there could easily be an encounter with native grasses or one of the boulders that line the driving area.

A second-shot layup is required to keep the ball short of another rock outcropping that also features low shrubs and rough grassland.

That leaves the player about 100 yards uphill to a very unique green that is set just in front of yet another outcropping of monster rocks. The green has two levels—the front section being quite narrow and the back portion being rather wide.

If the ball is resting on the very front of the green and the cup is placed either back right or back left, it will be impossible to putt directly at the hole.

Engh has made a habit of creating out-of-the-ordinary courses in the midst of dazzling settings, and Redlands Mesa ranks among his very best.

DRINKER DURRANCE GRAPHICS

Glenwood Springs, Colorado's, Drinker Durrance Graphics provided much of the stunning photography for *Spectacular Golf of Colorado*. The firm's partners have taken some of the most breathtaking photography around the world, from national parks to natural/fine art to golf.

For over 22 years, Susan G. Drinker has been a professional photographer, though her passion for the craft began in childhood. Nationally and internationally honored and recognized, in 1991 Susan became the first woman ever awarded a Marlboro assignment. Her panoramic images can be seen on posters, postcards and fine art throughout the world and in fine books.

Dick Durrance II launched his unusually diverse career in Vietnam, photographing combat. Following seven years as a staff photographer for National Geographic, Dick spent the next 12 years as an advertising photographer. Today he documents magnificent golf courses throughout the world.

The White House News Photographers Association named him their "Magazine Photographer of the Year" in 1972, and the American Society of Media Photographers awarded him their "Advertising Photographer of the Year" title in 1987. In 2004, he was one of four photographers selected as a Founding Member of the Academy for Golf Art.

Susan and Dick expertly blend the ethereal beauty of the outdoors while capturing the reality of the moment. *Spectacular Golf of Colorado* proudly displays their illustrious works of art.

Photograph by Jules Alexander

Photograph by Dick Durrance II

DRINKER DURRANCE GRAPHICS
Dick Durrance II
Sue Drinker
725 Elk Springs Drive
Glenwood Springs, Colorado 81601
970.945.5666
Fax 970.945.5679
www.drinkerdurrance.com

Wilson
ROOKIE

The Colorado PGA Foundation is dedicated to bringing the enjoyment of the game of golf to all while preserving its rich history and tradition in Colorado.

Created and founded by the Colorado Section PGA, the Colorado PGA Foundation is committed to providing opportunities to better communities through golf—a game established on the values of honesty, integrity, respect, responsibility, confidence and judgment.

The Colorado PGA Foundation looks to support community-minded organizations that work to meet their mission through these ideals and the game of golf.

Through the development of the Colorado PGA Historical Center and support of the Colorado Golf Hall of Fame, the Colorado PGA Foundation is committed to preserving the history of golf in Colorado and ensuring the sport retains a relevant place in the lives of those who enjoy its attributes.

Through community support, scholarship programs, history preservation and growth of the game programs, the Colorado PGA Foundation strives to impact individuals' lives through the game of golf by bettering communities, promoting strong values and character development and instilling lifelong ideals.

COLORADO SECTION

Colorado PGA Foundation
6630 Bear Dance Road, Suite 200
Larkspur, Colorado 80118
303.681.0742
Fax 303.681.2742
www.coloradopga.com

PUBLISHING TEAM

Brian G. Carabet, Publisher
John A. Shand, Publisher
Tom Fischer, Associate Publisher
Elizabeth Fischer, Associate Publisher

Michele Cunningham-Scott, Art Director
Mary Elizabeth Acree, Graphic Designer
Emily Kattan, Graphic Designer
Ben Quintanilla, Graphic Designer

Elizabeth Gionta, Managing Editor
Rosalie Wilson, Editor
Lauren Castelli, Editor
Anita Kasmar, Editor
Michael Rabun, Contributing Editor
Braden Hanson, Premier Aerials Photography, Contributing Photographer

Kristy Randall, Senior Production Coordinator
Laura Greenwood, Production Coordinator
Jennifer Lenhart, Production Coordinator
Jessica Garrison, Traffic Coordinator

Carol Kendall, Project Manager
Beverly Smith, Project Manager

PANACHE PARTNERS, LLC
CORPORATE OFFICE
13747 Montfort Drive
Suite 100
Dallas, TX 75240
972.661.9884
www.panache.com

COLORADO OFFICE
303.799.4244

Lakewood Country Club 13th Hole, Photograph by Premier Aerials Photography

ACKNOWLEDGEMENTS

As we began our journey in selecting the most spectacular golf holes in Colorado, we quickly concluded that we needed input from people who have made Colorado golf their livelihood. Ron Ruscio, one of the primary photographers for our book *Dream Homes of Colorado* introduced us to Tom Ferrell, president of Denver-based OnTour Media, which produces broadcast, retail and commercial video products for the golf industry. We met with Tom in the spring of 2006 to discuss forming an advisory group to help us identify and select which golf courses to feature in this book. Through Tom's assistance, we reached out to Colorado PGA Executive Director Darrell Bock, golf-course architect Rick Phelps and *Colorado AvidGolfer* magazine editor Jon Rizzi. Over the summer and into the fall, we met several times with the group to review our progress and to solicit new ideas. The group was instrumental in our partnering with photographer Dick Durrance II, whose images grace many of these pages.

Each of these individuals brought an authoritative and impassioned perspective informed by their positions. In his role as executive director of the Colorado Section of the PGA of America, Darrell Bock presides over the 750 PGA golf professionals at more than 280 courses across Colorado and in parts of Wyoming and South Dakota. It's a sure bet that nearly half of those layouts bear the fingerprints of Rick Phelps, who with his father, Richard Phelps, and business partner, Kevin Atkinson, make up Phelps/Atkinson Golf Design, the Evergreen-based firm credited with more than 300 projects nationwide. Tom Ferrell has written about the game played on Rick's and others' courses in books such as *The Scramblers Dozen*, with 1999 PGA Teacher of the Year Mike McGetrick, and has won national magazine awards for his instructional articles and profiles. In addition to running OnTour, Tom is editor-at-large for *Colorado AvidGolfer*, the state's leading golf and lifestyle magazine founded and edited by Jon Rizzi, whose 25 years of publishing experience at such titles as *Esquire, ESPN* and *Travel & Leisure Golf* helped shape this paean to Colorado golf.

Tom & Elizabeth Fischer

Advisory Board for Spectacular Golf of Colorado. *Pictured (from left to right): Jon Rizzi, Editor of* Colorado AvidGolfer *magazine; Darrell Bock, Executive Director of the Colorado Section of the PGA of America; Rick Phelps, Golf Course Architect and Co-owner of Phelps/Atkinson Golf Design; Not pictured: Tom Ferrell, President of OnTour Media.*

Photograph by Dana McGrath

INDEX